starting out with style

DESIGN SOLUTIONS FOR YOUR NEW HOME

edited by Monica Millward Weeks

SALT LAKE CITY

First Edition
05 04 03 02 01 5 4 3 2 1

Jacket photos: All photos courtesy of Room & Board/Retrospect except Mission-style bedroom (back cover), courtesy of Living.com.
Opposite page, left to right: Photos courtesy of Room & Board, Retrospect, and Living.com.
Page vi: Photo courtesy of Living.com.

Published by
Gibbs Smith, Publisher
P.O. Box 667
Layton, Utah 84041

Orders: (800) 748-5439
www.gibbs-smith.com

Edited by Monica Millward Weeks
Designed and produced by FORTHGEAR, Inc.
Printed and bound in Korea

Library of Congress Cataloging-in-Publication Data

Starting out with style : design solutions for your new home / edited by Monica Millward Weeks.—1st ed.
p. cm.
ISBN 1-58685-097-0
1. Interior decoration. I. Weeks, Monica Millward. II. Gibbs Smith, Publisher.
NK2115 .S66 2001
747—dc21
2001001183

contents

introduction

Welcome to *Starting Out with Style*—a beginner's guide to decorating your house or apartment.

You've plunked down the cash, signed the papers, and the key is in your hand—you've finally moved into a place of your very own. If you're lucky, you might have a futon and some hand-me-down furniture from Mom and Dad. If you're less lucky, you might be thinking up ways to decorate with cardboard boxes! Maybe you have a budget to splurge on new furnishings, or you might have to make the most of what you already have. Whatever your circumstances, you want a place that says, "This is my house…not my mom's, not Martha Stewart's, but mine!" You've got a few ideas, but how do you know where to start?

Enter *Starting Out with Style*—a guide to decorating your house from scratch. Within these pages you'll find no-nonsense advice on evaluating your tastes, personality, and lifestyle to create a home that fits you, including information about different styles and color schemes. If you don't know the difference between Art Deco and Arts & Crafts, the chapter "What's My Style?" will not only educate you about different styles but help you evaluate which styles will work best for you. The "Common Sense Design" chapter will show you how to put these styles to work as you plan your design from floor to ceiling.

Next we'll walk you through each room, outlining decorating options and detailing choices for furnishings, flooring, lighting, windows, and walls throughout the home. We'll discuss ideas for living areas, kitchen and dining areas, bedrooms, bathrooms, and home offices, with full-color photographs illustrating a variety of styles.

For first-time homeowners or renters, the practical solutions included will help you deal with budget limitations, living in small spaces, personalizing your space, and coping with rental restrictions, as well as help you bone up on thrift-store and flea-market shopping skills. The extensive resource guide will lead you to a wide variety of shopping destinations, including many Internet resources. Whatever your tastes, *Starting Out with Style* will inspire you to create a pad with personality.

—Monica Millward Weeks, Editor

naked flowers exposed

what's my style?

Okay, so you know what you like, or at least you know it when you see it. Maybe you've been living with hand-me-downs from Mom and Dad for a few years, and now you're ready to furnish your place in the style you want. But how do you begin transforming your tastes into a real, living style for your home? With all of the styles out there, it can be confusing to know where to start. These explanations of various styles, provided by interior designers from Kozyhome, will help you begin to dissect the wide world of style and help you figure out what your tastes are.

This contemporary living room manages to be casually elegant by pairing velvety sofas with sturdy wood tables. Photo courtesy of Living.com.

Something Old

Do you love antiques? Does the idea of digging through Grandma's attic to find treasures for your place thrill you? Do you fantasize about living in an old farmhouse, a palace, or even a castle? If you answered "yes" to any of these questions, try one or more of these styles:

TRADITIONAL

Keynotes of this style are classic shapes, forms, and textures. Woods are predominantly cherry, mahogany, satin wood, and walnut, finished in a rich brown or reddish-brown patina. Certain periods have beautifully painted furniture, with lacquer finishes such as black, Chinese red, or emerald green. A more natural-looking finish, called a pickled finish, appears in oak or pine furnishings from the Georgian and Colonial periods.

Hardwood floors and oriental rugs complement the traditional style well. Window treatments include simple curtains, valances, heavy swags, and jabots. Fabrics come in a wide range of palettes, predominantly displaying jewel tones. They can have small motifs or large floral patterns. Fabrics incorporated are silks, tapestries, brocades, damasks, and velvets. More casual traditional rooms often include plaids. Traditional wall coverings encompass molding, wallpaper, fabrics, and *trompe l'oeil* painting. Sub-styles within the traditional are Biedermeir, Victorian, Regency, Federal, Louis XV, Directoire, or Empire. These sub-styles can lend distinctive character to a

This elegant curio cabinet is likely to be discovered within the walls of a traditional home. Photo courtesy of Pulaski Furniture.

The vintage look can be seen in this romantic bedroom, which features a curvaceous wicker bed draped in Victorian-style linens. Photo courtesy of Highland House/Thomasville.

The comfort of country style is evident in this living room, which is wrapped in yellow and white and splashed in blue floral accents. Photo courtesy of Living.com.

The sleek lines and rich oak texture of this dining set are characteristic of Mission style, a regional subset of Arts & Crafts design. Photo courtesy of Living.com.

Pine furnishings combined with handcrafted accessories and comfortable linens make up this cozy farmhouse-style bedroom. Photo courtesy of Living.com.

traditional interior. (If you want to learn more about these sub-styles, check out a book that specializes in French or English historical styles.)

VINTAGE

The Victorian-inspired vintage style also includes Art Deco and Art Nouveau elements. This style is rooted in historic traditions with a romantic and feminine feel. Classic features also add to transitional or country interiors, and can soften a rustic design. Long fringe, flowing lines, bent-wood furniture, overstuffed cushions, and fringed and tasseled borders all find a place in the vintage style. Their nature is often reflected in motifs and *objets d'art*.

FARMHOUSE/COUNTRY

The farmhouse style encompasses country designs including regional English and French country. Key elements of farmhouse style include mellow woods, such as pine or oak, painted or stained furniture, handwoven rugs, stoneware, china, and embroidery. Furniture and furnishings range from genuine antiques to flea market treasures to contemporary pieces that incorporate the appropriate textures, colors, and woods. Versatile and unpretentious, it is relatively inexpensive with a handcrafted look. The farmhouse/country style mixes well with other styles, from neoclassic to modern. Furniture pieces are often functional, adding charm and highlighting individuality. Nostalgic keepsakes, pottery, memorabilia, dolls, or old tools might be featured in a country environment.

RUSTIC

Rustic style's distinctive characteristics include homespun crafts, do-it-yourself items, simple shapes, and unpretentious materials. The versatile, simple furniture mixes easily with other styles, especially neoclassic and contemporary. Hammer marks or natural distressing in the finish of these wooden pieces add a sense of individuality and handmade quality. The comfortable, subdued upholstery may have earth-tone textures or tea-stained floral patterns. The rustic room offers a warm ambiance and an invitation to relax. Sometimes rustic environments are flavored with a regional flair, such as southwestern, Scandinavian, or Mexican.

ARTS AND CRAFTS

Arts and Crafts, a historical style, encompasses mission, modern craftsman, and country styles. Natural materials, such as stone, glazed tile, copper, bronze, and dark wood tones—oak particularly—typify this style. Its distinctive stylistic feature is rectilinear lines and massive proportions, simple geometric cutouts, and copper or bronze hardware. Geometric motifs and design restraint make the Arts and Crafts style highly compatible with modern and contemporary styles of the twentieth century. Architecturally inspired, this design's size and proportion give it a masculine feel. Fabrics are often textures, geometrics, or small-scale stylized flowers and leaves in soft pale-green, blue, and brown hues.

This traditional living room set features luxurious furnishings wrapped in leather and velvet, two textures frequently found in traditional homes. Photo courtesy of Living.com.

The clean lines and modern look of this sofa and chair pairing are based on mid-twentieth-century design. Their neutral colors and quiet elegance are representative of modern style. Photo courtesy of Room & Board.

This bedroom is a modern adaptation of the Art Deco look, featuring streamlined furnishings with dramatic angles. Photo courtesy of Furniture.com.

OTHER HISTORICAL DESIGN GENRES

Historical design eras include eighteenth-century, Arts and Crafts, Victorian, Queen Anne, neoclassic, and contemporary. National or regional styles, such as southwestern, English country, or Caribbean were either developed or popularized in specific geographic areas. Historic styles refer to the design of the period, such as Baroque, neoclassic, and Louis XV, while other styles are named for influential designers or schools of design. Chippendale, Hepplewhite, and Bauhaus are among the list. Twentieth-century styles include Art Nouveau, Art Moderne, art deco, high tech, and minimalist.

Something New

Are you the type to discard old clothes and furnishings in favor of the latest styles? Do you seek out the newest gadgets as soon as they hit the market? Do you prefer a sleek, uncluttered look for your home? If you find yourself nodding in agreement, check out what these styles have to offer.

MODERN

Driven by architects, the modern style uses industrial materials and clean, even austere, lines, shapes, and colors. The modern color palette is neutral and monochromatic, using blacks and browns for drama and definition. Splashes of color, constrained within art collections or smaller

This graceful settee and tea table bring the beauty of the French countryside to this sunny sitting room. Photo courtesy of Highland House/Thomasville.

upholstered items, can also highlight a modern room. Modern furniture tends to be sophisticated and streamlined, with an emphasis on nickel or chrome, mirrors, and glass.

Horizontal lines take precedence over vertical dimensions, while curvilinear lines create a self-contained, structural-looking movement. Bleached and pickled woods with Berber rugs typify the modern style. Typically viewed as a colder design style, a modern room invites human interaction. The stillness and quiet of modern rooms warms the moment people arrive. Orderly, expansive design creates a backdrop for lively conversation and entertaining activities.

CONTEMPORARY

Contemporary style embodies the maxim "form follows function," with texture, color, and comfort as its keynotes. This is a style that emphasizes simplicity, warmth, and neatness. An intriguing mix of textures contrast with sleek surfaces, such as marble, glass, metal, and acrylics. Upholstery and accent fabrics such as leather, suede, raw silk, wool, and linen provide contrast to the cool lines and surface finishes. The occasional antique or *objet d'art* adds interest and personality to the room. Contemporary style is also versatile, mixing easily with most other styles.

The rich mahogany wood and damask upholstery keep this dining room firmly rooted in the traditional, but the flowing lines of the set, along with the leopard-spotted rug, give the room a contemporary kick. Photo courtesy of Living.com.

This Asian-style mahogany living room set creates harmony with its clean, simple lines and solid construction. Photo courtesy of Zencraft.

Don't Fence Me In!

But maybe you don't fit into either category—perhaps you're attracted to lots of different styles, or maybe you'd rather create your own style. If that's the case, learn more about these styles that keep an open mind about things both old and new.

TRANSITIONAL

Transitional designs possess elements of two distinct styles. Usually, a transitional design is rooted in the traditional and moves toward the more casual and contemporary. Blending past with present, transitional environments arrange furnishings in a more traditional or formal manner, while fabrics, accessories, and specific furniture pieces create a warm, relaxed ambiance. This provides clean lines softened with comfort and familiarity. Transitional rooms are uncluttered yet personable.

Whether traditional or period architecture showcases more contemporary or eclectic furnishings, or contemporary architecture provides a backdrop for traditional upholstery and furniture, the two styles can combine and complement one another for a beautiful home. Transitional fabrics and colors are comfortable and relaxed plaids, solids, or stylized florals, adding to the comfortable, inviting atmosphere. Window treatments range from planter shutters and simple drapery to nothing at all, depending on the desire and need for privacy.

ECLECTIC

Eclectic style combines several design periods with an improvisational feel. It occurs quite naturally as people living in a household bring their distinct preferences and tastes to their environment. These rooms may feel more global or international in tone, juxtaposing contemporary upholstery and ethnic crafts. A common color palette brings together the various elements harmoniously. Many designers have made their careers with the eclectic style by mixing various periods of architecture, furniture, and accessories. The key to creating a successful eclectic interior lies in having self-confidence and a passion for bold experimentation, balanced by a strong sense of form, scale, and color.

An African-themed living room fuses elements of traditional, rustic, and contemporary style. Photo courtesy of Waverly.

An intriguing wall tapestry and tasteful rug help to transform this bedroom into a courtly European-style retreat. Photo courtesy of Guy Chaddock and Company.

CHAPTER 2

common sense design

Now that you have identified what styles you like best, it's time to figure out where to begin transforming your space to match your taste. Should you start with the walls, the ceiling, or the furniture? How do you combine different styles to create a unique look? What about accessories? Advice from interior designers at ImproveNet.com, Designviews, and IHome.com will show you how to translate your ideas into design solutions for your apartment or home.

Decorative accents lend charm to a room, as witnessed by this collection of Asian mementos on a bedside table. Photo: Trisha Ison.

Taking the Mystery Out of Interior Design

by Arlene Claiborne
courtesy of ImproveNet.com

If you love to study design magazines but freeze when it comes to trying those ideas in your own home, then you'll warm up to this simple, step-by-step approach to home decorating.

Rather than trying to tackle the whole room at once, start by breaking down each room into its basic building components: floors, ceilings, walls, doors, windows, and architectural details. Determining the selections for each of these components will set the tone and character of the room. That, in turn, will dictate the style of furniture, lighting, window treatments, and accessories needed to complete the room's point of view. For specific ideas in each of these areas, check out the message boards at www.improvenet.com, which feature advice from design pros as well as from other homeowners.

Start with the floor. Along with the ceiling, the floor represents the largest share of space in the room, although it's actually more important, since we come in direct contact with the floor. Any steps and staircases in the room should be included as well. How will the room be used? Are you looking for soft carpet so you can get down and play with the kids, or elegant parquet flooring? Once you determine the type of flooring that will work best in the space, start considering colors. Will light colors stand up to the traffic? Will dark colors show pet hair? Do you want the room to look serene and calm in cooler hues, or festive and bright in warmer tones?

Arranged to maximize the space in this living room, these cozy, overstuffed white sofas are perfect for entertaining. Photo courtesy of Bassett Furniture.

furniture arranging

The move is finally over, but now you're left with a jumble of furniture in the center of the room. Where on earth are you going to put all of that stuff? Here are a few tips for arranging furniture:

- **Draw it out on paper first.** You don't have to be an artist—even a sketchy outline will help you visualize your furniture placement. If you want to get really detailed, grab a tape measure and measure the room and furniture, and then draw the room to scale on graph paper. This may seem like a hassle, but it will save you the effort of dragging your sofa across the room four times until you get it right.
- **Get comfortable.** This is especially important in a new place—be sure to get a feel for the room before you make any major decisions. Do you gravitate to one part of the room to lounge about? Is there a natural focal point, like a fireplace? How do the windows and doors affect the room's layout? As you consider these things, you'll get a better idea of how your furnishings will fit into the room.
- **Start with the big stuff.** Chances are that smaller furnishings will fall easily into place once you position larger pieces like beds and sofas.
- **Clear a path.** Don't forget that you'll actually have to walk through your rooms. Be sure to leave plenty of space for pathways (at least two-and-a-half feet), or even large rooms will start to feel cramped.
- **Keep an open mind.** Consider pulling furnishings away from the wall, or placing them at an angle. And consider alternate uses for objects—maybe a bedside table will fit perfectly under that narrow window in the kitchen.

This sideboard and china hutch combine European-style design with a rustic flair. Mexican accessories help to create a truly multicultural room. Photo courtesy of Segusino/Marina's.

The ceiling should be the next thing to consider. Many ceilings are simple, neutral areas. If a large expanse of blank ceiling looks just plain boring, you can break up the space with details that complement the flooring. Ceiling light fixtures, fans, or even skylights can add interest. Don't be afraid to consider painting your ceiling; you can always repaint it if you change your mind. Start a shade or two lighter than the chip you like since color intensifies on a larger area. Test your color choice by brushing out a four-by-four-foot section and looking at the color under different light at different times of day.

Wall materials and their finishes are third on the list. Wall options tend to be the most overwhelming, but if you've already made your decisions on the flooring and ceiling, it should be easier to narrow your choices. Paint is always the safest decision using the testing guidelines suggested above. You can get more variety and personality with borders and stenciling or faux finishes, without committing to wallpaper. Don't forget to consider wall lighting as well, and how the light will create its own detailing on the wall.

Consider architectural detailing for ceilings, walls, windows, and doors at the same time. The style of molding choices around windows and doors should blend together, but it's not important to match everything perfectly. Some detailing in the room can be stained, while other elements can be painted in a coordinating tone or classic white finish.

Finally, consider furnishings, cabinets, and accessories. Once you've made your decisions on the major building components, furniture and cabinetry selections turn architectural space into personal space. Window treatments should be chosen after the furniture is selected, considering light quality, privacy requirements, and, finally, color.

Last on the list for interior design choices are decorative accents and accessories. These charmers give a room its individuality and can be constantly refreshed with new finds and ideas. Remember, the most beautiful homes are never "done" but always evolving, and that's what makes decorating your home so much fun!

Author profile: Arlene Claiborne owned an interior design firm in the Baltimore, Maryland, area for ten years. There she participated in several Decorator Show Houses. Also during that time, she opened a retail art studio/gallery called Shagreen, which showcased painted furniture. She holds an interior design degree from the University of Maryland.

Easy Mixing

courtesy of Designviews.com

With so many great items and combinations today, there is no reason any home should look like another. The days of a generic off-the-rack look are over. Access to items of every style and description has never been greater. Your sense of style and comfort and your personality should be obvious everywhere. Forget what the neighbors have—dare to be different. After all, there is nothing duller than absolute perfection.

Unexpected touches add a sense of spirit. Experiment a little—often the smallest touches can give big results. A whimsical pillow on a pedigreed couch, a picture you drew when you were five, funky lamps in a serious dining room, anything that makes you smile—no home is complete without these.

These days, the eclectic look is in. You see it in magazine spreads all the time. It looks so inviting, so comfortable . . . so good. Just throw a bunch of styles together and it will look great, right? How hard could it be? Not hard at all, if you follow these basic guidelines for combining styles with ease.

Don't Create a Museum

Total dedication to any one style can be tempting. After all, it seems hard to get it wrong. But reproductions of any one style or period usually come off cold and constrained. Unless you're going for the historic preservation award, it pays to mix. Balance and harmony come from contrast, and combining two or more styles allows them to play off each other. Contrasting styles bring a room to life, give it personality, and create a comfortable, enjoyable environment. Not locking into one style also dramatically improves your home's ability to outlive trends.

Country and mission styles are easy to mix, as they both celebrate natural materials. This living room combines a Mission-style coffee table with a comfortable country-style sofa and chair. Photo courtesy of Living.com.

artfully accenting your home

courtesy of IHome.com

Creating the ideal home décor is like putting together the consummate outfit. You've already got the foundation—great shoes, a fabulous dress, but there's something missing. You need some finishing touches to set off the whole look and make it complete . . . you need accessories!

We all know how the perfect piece of jewelry can be the icing on the cake of a fashion ensemble, and the same can be said of decorative accessories for the home. Candles, vases, picture frames, and other home accent products can add the missing elements to a décor that bring it all together. Use them to create a unique look by adding pieces that reflect your individuality and signature style.

Decorative objects can instantly add interest to any room, just by how they are displayed. The art of "table scaping" is picturing your bedside table, coffee table, and other furniture as blank canvases on which to decorate with a variety of shapes, textures, and colors. The key to elegant displays is the lushness of the layering. Choose items that are functional as well as appealing to the eye. Juxtaposing items of varying scale—stacking a collection of books or grouping a set of decorative boxes—can turn what could be a messy tabletop into an artful presentation.

If you think of your table as a setting for a still life, you can create visually pleasing looks that will enhance your décor. Candles and candleholders of different heights lend soft light and subtle aroma (if they're scented) to a room as well as making beautiful centerpieces for any table. Use decorative accents to grace a mantel or bookshelf—a stylish vase, or picture frame holding a cherished photo—elements that add personality to a décor with their subtle charm.

Attention to the smaller details in any space is a large part of what makes your home unique and special. Change accessories for each new season to give an affordable fresh look to your décor. Be creative and have fun dressing up your home!

Limit Yourself to Two or Three Styles

Some designers can mix a handful of styles and pull it off beautifully. But unless you have the eye and the instinct for it, your number one rule should be to limit yourself to two or three styles. Some guidelines that work:

- 70% one style - (Country, for example)
- 30% contrasting style - (Industrial, for example)

Another easy approach:

- 60% one style - (Asian, for example)
- 30% similar style - (mission, for example)
- 10% contrasting style - (African, for example)

The exact percentages are unimportant if you get the basic rule—one style or two similar styles should dominate. Some people prefer to leave out the contrasting style and get the contrast from certain materials, such as a metal chair in a room filled with soft natural fibers and colors. And if you find yourself with more than three styles, at least simplify your palette. Painting everything similar colors will unify a diverse group of furnishings.

This collection of vintage dolls and marionettes, placed high atop an armoire, adds an air of whimsy to this bedroom. Photo: Trisha Ison.

Books are the ultimate home accent, showcased here on these curvy bookcases. Photo courtesy of Crate & Barrel.

Use the Either/or Principle

Contrast can come from more than opposing styles: the house itself, a fabric, or the line of a chair can all serve to create a modern edge. Your goal here is not to contrast everything individually, but to provide overall contrast or focal points. An easy guideline is the either/or principle:

> Either a contemporary home filled with classics, or a historic home with contemporary furnishings.
>
> Either a big, full curtain in a humble fabric or a simple flat shade in a luxurious material.
>
> Either a bold-colored backdrop for a neutral palette, or a neutral backdrop filled with colorful furnishings.
>
> Either contemporary art in a traditional room or old masters in a modern setting.

GARDENING

African-style sculptures are reflected in a sleek mirror, creating a serene setting. Photo courtesy of Crate & Barrel.

The oversized sofa and wicker chaise lounge give this room a relaxed and casual French country feel. Photo courtesy of Retrospect.

show your true colors

By now you probably have an idea of what you want your home or apartment to look like. But don't forget to consider the most important element of all—color! Color gives life to a room, adding a welcoming touch to any look. Whatever your style, the use of color can make or break your home's design scheme. Whether you favor bright colors or more muted tones, here's some advice that will guide you in the right direction.

The cool whites and blues in the walls and furnishings establish country charm in this cozy home office. Photo courtesy of Crate & Barrel.

Crazy for Color

courtesy of Furniture.com

Color is everywhere—in nature, on television and computers, at work, and at restaurants. You can't help loving color, embracing it, and expecting it. "Since the '60s, we've had more significant experiences with color," says Margaret Walch, director of the Color Association of the United States. "People in their twenties grew up with color and expect whatever they want to be available in the color they want. I remember having to accept color, going to buy a car and the only option was gray. It's now a matter of color expectation."

So why are so many bedrooms still blah beige and living rooms as neutral as Switzerland? Perhaps it's time to take advantage of all the color that's out there and welcome it into our homes. After all, "color adds life and interest," reminds Walch. And with a little advice from experts, it's easier than you may think to take color by the horns and tame it for your home.

The Rule of Three

"Most people are afraid to use too many colors, but what they often fail to see is that it's the way they use and place color that can make or break the room," says Furniture.com design consultant Margaret Sheldon, who proposes an easy "rule of three" that can help infuse your home with vitality.

Decorate your space with tiers of color. Begin with a rug, fabric, or wallpaper you love and look closely at what colors are in it. "The rug is a good place to start because it warms the room and you can build up," suggests Sheldon. "You want the color you choose to appear three times in the room. For example, in the rug, in the drapes or sofa fabric, and then in an accent like throw pillows, decorative balls, or even a mantel's candlesticks. Mantels are a great place because they're at eye level."

Accents are an easy, inexpensive way to add color to an interior that needs a boost. Colored pillows or a chenille throw stylishly draped over your sofa are simple but powerful design solutions. Area rugs, vases, and even fresh flowers are other options you can easily add and change to match your mood.

The Front End of the Rainbow (or Where to Begin)

Color is personal. You need to select home colors that you like and can live with. Consider these questions:

- **What colors are already in the room?** Do you have a favorite piece of furniture, fabric, or rug? If you already like a color, it's a great starting point, because you know you can live with it. If your favorite piece has a pattern, look closely: it can give you clues as to what colors work well together and in what proportions.

- **What colors do I love?** What colors make me happy? If you don't have an immediate answer to this question, check your closet. Does one color dominate? Design consultant Sheldon, who is trained as an architect, was recently working with a client to choose wall colors for a new house. After finally finding the perfect bedroom color, the client realized it was the same shade as her favorite coat. When you like a color, you really like a color. (However, we must suggest this tactic with a bit of caution. It rarely works for men, who often have a limited range of color behind those closet doors.

Shades of blue and silver mesh to create an easy sophistication in this bedroom. Photo courtesy of Crate & Barrel.

It is entirely possible for someone to be passionate about green and have nary a green garment in view.)

❖ **Keep your eyes open**—beautiful color and color combinations are all around you. Home magazines, stores, and restaurants are good places to explore your palette preferences and can help you see how colors work together. Think of places that you enjoy and how their décor and color scheme contribute to your pleasure.

"When you're a kid, you pick a favorite color and you always buy the same color of lollipop at the store. As an adult, when you buy sheets, you probably stick to the same color families and tones. It's an instinct. You should pay attention to that," advises Edmund Wise, another design consultant at Furniture.com.

Creating Your Environment

Colors have both visual and psychological effects on how you feel. People react differently to colors, just as they like and dislike certain foods. Even colors in the same family can evoke very different responses. For example, lime, forest, and sage green each bring a distinctive tone and attitude to an interior while having the same base color. Greens, like other cool colors, make rooms feel lighter and bigger. Although these hues can feel cold on their own, they can have a dramatic effect when combined with other colors. Most greens lend a quiet tranquility and, in dark hues, recall the richness of nature. Use this color in kitchens, bathrooms, living rooms, dining rooms, patios, and anyplace else you want a sense of the great outdoors. Light blue adds airiness and evokes the sky, perfect for bedrooms, bathrooms, and any other space for relaxing. Rich blues allude to night skies and create deep, quiet drama; turquoise freshens up a space, clearing your mind and aiding in communication—a good choice for small rooms, bedrooms, bathrooms and studies.

These black leather roadster chairs add exceptional style and a vintage flair to this living room. Photo courtesy of Room & Board.

color clues

Lighting affects color, so be sure to get lots of samples (you can always whittle down) and look at the colors and textures in the room's lighting. Colors reflect and absorb each other, so try to view them together, especially if you are adding to already existing elements. When picking paint, brush some on a piece of poster board and position it near your furnishings and/or wallpaper to see how it all looks together.

Reds, oranges, and yellows add warmth to a space and make an interior cozier. Red is better for small spaces and finishing touches than for large areas. Because it stimulates your metabolism and neural development, bright red is a good accent choice for kitchens and exercise rooms, while deep reds work well in dining and living rooms. Pink is more nurturing and encourages rest and relaxation. Try it in bedrooms and other spaces where therapeutic and tranquil feelings are the goal.

Orange can offer an upbeat, supportive, and friendly tone. Try it in kitchens, studies, halls, living rooms, and dining rooms. Peach tones, which make everyone look good regardless of skin coloring, are terrific for any room where you want your guests to look their best. Yellow adds the warm energy of a sunny day. This mentally stimulating color is suitable for living rooms, dining rooms, family rooms, and kitchens. A creamy yellow adds a bit of life to bedrooms and studies without being overwhelming.

You'll want to be sure you can live with violets, purples, and magentas—a little bit goes a long way. These colors create rich cocoons that are warm but very powerful. Try them in bedrooms, entrances, studies, and meditation spaces.

These sage green sofas create a serene setting for reading or for comfortable conversation. Photo courtesy of Living.com.

This yellow armchair is perfect for a sunny spot next to the window. Photo courtesy of Lexington.

White, black, brown, gray, gold, and silver are all neutral colors, most often used to contrast and highlight cool and warm colors. Black tends to make spaces appear smaller; brown conveys earth, nurturing and warmth; gold adds sparkle and inspiration; and silver signifies change, coolness, and femininity. But mixing neutrals does not always result in a dreary monotonous scheme. In fact, contrasting dark and light neutrals can create a sophisticated, understated look, recalling modern and oriental designs. Even pale neutrals can be used together for a Zen-like effect. And mixing it up where textures are concerned can make your rooms that much more luxurious. Just remember, confidence and a love of color can go a long way together.

Whatever color you choose or however bold or subtle you decide to go, color is about personal style. "Luckily, furniture is so transitional today, incorporating traditional motifs with more modern appeal, that people may comfortably work with nearly any color range they like," notes Wise. "As long as they are coordinating colors and patterns, they will be able to create a living space that is ideal for them."

More Color Points to Consider

courtesy of Designviews.com

Consider Room Dimensions

"Small rooms should be white or light" can practically be considered a nasty rumor at this point. It may work for you and your color scheme, but it's no hard and fast rule. Often the reverse is true. A small room will never be a big room. Embrace it for what it is and choose another adjective—cozy, dramatic, decadent, or exotic, for instance. If the illusion of space is your biggest objective, the lack of overall contrast is the biggest factor. Color wrapping works especially well in small rooms—selecting the same color for walls, ceiling, and flooring creates the impression of a larger space.

This handsome armoire is actually a three-piece home entertainment center. The dramatic green tones were created by layering a series of paint coats and textures on the wood. Photo courtesy of Habersham.

In large rooms, the most critical decision is whether to play the size up or down. Again, if your objective is the feeling of space, keep your background consistent. A large room, however, may need to be scaled down to more human dimensions. Choose contrasting wall and floor colors, or keep a consistent background and group furniture into functional areas differentiated by color.

Consider Your Region

The region of the country where you live should be a consideration when selecting colors for your décor, but people often place too much emphasis here. That's one reason why you see so much "cloning" in certain parts of the country. Certainly, a city apartment surrounded by urban gray poses a different set of challenges than a mountaintop retreat or a midwest suburban ranch; however, this does not lock you into a set traditional color palette. Consider the climate and lighting of your region and then select the colors appropriate for your home and your lifestyle.

All of the colors you see when you view a room (which includes outdoor views) need to be considered, as does the amount and quality of light, which can vary dramatically from one area of a country to another. In south Florida, for instance, cool colors may be preferable as a respite from the warm southern sun. In the Northeast, you may need a sunny warm wall color to get you through the winter.

A good rule of thumb to follow is to allow a broader set of color choices as you move from the outside in. The colors for the exterior of your home should certainly take into account the adjoining homes and the feel and period of your neighborhood. But once you move inside, your choices should expand. Colors should flow and harmonize throughout your home, but no one should be dictating your bedroom colors but you!

Consider Decorating Style

Almost every decorating style has colors with which it is closely associated. Some styles even imply certain colors—the earth tones of natural style, for example. Art deco has its palette of strong pastels; nautical style thrives on red, white, and blue; and tropical style usually brings to mind bright bold hues. But you're not stuck with all of them. In fact, nothing may make your personal mix look fresher than an unexpected color! A bold iris blue in a traditional antiques-filled home or a pale chartreuse backdrop for a mix of African and mid-century modern pieces can give a modern vitality.

Nautical can be updated using sea green and turquoise, tropical revived with a monochromatic color scheme using a range of subtly different shades within the same hue. In fact, almost every style can be modernized by varying the color palette. This isn't a no-holds-barred tactic; common sense should prevail. Bright blue and red stripes will never work in a Zen-like retreat. The point is to stretch your color conceptions—not work against the style you want to achieve.

A comfortable brown velvet couch paired with a bamboo chair and ottoman creates visual harmony, producing an elegant living room. Photo courtesy of Pottery Barn.

Adding Flair to Your Lair

Sure, you can design your room to look exactly like that magazine layout you saw in *House Beautiful* last month (well, at least you could if you had the cash!) But why copy someone else's design when you have a decorator lurking inside of you, just dying to get out? The key to having a home that you love is adding some of your own personality to it. Whether you live in a spacious home or a tiny studio apartment, you can add personal touches in a variety of ways.

- ❖ Don't throw those interior design magazines away just yet. Seeking inspiration from professional designs is a great place to start. Check out rooms in magazines, books, and television shows, as well as every room you walk into. What do you like about each room you see? Think about how you can put your own twist on the styles you see.

- ❖ Personalize it! If you love winter sports, hang antique skis or ice skates on the wall. If you're a bookworm, accessorize by displaying books with cool covers. If you're an aspiring photographer, hang up some of your photos. If you love it, show it off!

- ❖ Think theme—pick a theme for your room and run with it. Not only is it one of the easiest ways to decorate (by helping you narrow down your decorating choices), it can also be a lot of fun to search out items that will turn your living room into, say, a tropical island.

- ❖ Decorating for two? This can be a challenge, especially if your tastes run toward American country while he prefers a minimalist Zen look. Compromise by choosing furnishings that complement each of your styles—for example, a streamlined Arts & Crafts–style rocker might please both country and minimalist fans.

This collection of framed photos on a brightly-painted bookshelf shows off the personality of this home's occupant. Photo: Trisha Ison.

Another aspect to consider in your overall style and color scheme is what we call the immovable object. If it's not going anywhere, by all means take it into consideration. If the carpet is brown and there's no flooring budget in the foreseeable future, work with it, even if you hate it. Trying to pretend it isn't there will actually work against you. Every color can be improved by surrounding it with hues that enhance rather than detract. Consider any furniture that you already have, and consider painting some pieces to pull in your color even more. Flea-market style certainly lends itself to this approach. A whole room full of tag-sale finds can be unified by a single paint color or a subtle range of hues.

Consider—Do You Love It?

By far the most important consideration is choosing a color you love. Select a color that has relevance for you and that expresses something of your personality. Use your favorite color in at least one room. Obviously some colors lend themselves to this more than others. Bright orange is trendy and might be hard to live with throughout the house, but a few bold strokes in a room or two may be just the thing to make you smile. Or tone your chosen color down a notch—say, to a terra-cotta, which is a more livable color—and enjoy it in abundance. Some colors that seem difficult for interiors really aren't.

Not sure what you like? Keep a file with swatches, magazine pictures, and screen shots, and see which colors show up time and again. Whatever colors you do end up choosing, don't be afraid to use them liberally throughout the room. A room or two wrapped in color may be the breath of fresh air necessary to keep you happy with that closet full of neutrals.

These leather sofas provide classic style to this living room. The durability of leather makes it a great investment for your home. Photo courtesy of Ashley Furniture.

room by room

Now that you've got your style and colors in mind, it's time to look at each room in your home. From the living room to the bedroom, every room has a purpose, and it's important to take this into consideration while decorating. Asking yourself a series of questions about each room will help you figure out how to proceed: how often will you be using the room? What will you be using it for? How do you want to feel while you're in the room? For example, do you want your living room to be a cozy, relaxing escape from the world, or a lively den of entertainment? Your answers to these questions will help you determine what direction to take.

Many of us who are just starting out in life find ourselves in "starter" homes or apartments with limited space. If you have a small house or apartment, you may want to consider using rooms for more than one purpose: a guest bedroom/home office, kitchen/dining room, or bathroom/laundry room. We'll discuss how to work with small living spaces on page 112.

Advice from designers at Furniture.com, ImproveNet.com, WestpointStevens.com, and Kitchen-Bath.com will walk you through every major room of your house, helping you to make the most out of each room.

The New Living Room

courtesy of Furniture.com

It used to be that the living room was where you entertained guests, displayed valuables, or showed off your tastes, but it was never a place where you just lived. But as surely as style follows function, the look of living rooms is changing. They are now easy, welcoming, usually in proximity to the kitchen or home office, and filled with colors, fibers, furniture, and fabrics that reflect their new status.

Sofas, always the centerpiece of living room furniture, remain the focal point in rooms designed for casual living. Leather seating is popular, as are slipcovered sofas and chairs—a style that's both current and a wonderful nod to the past. The popularity of slipcovered furniture is obvious when rooms are used for everything from formal entertaining to video games. Versatile and practical slipcovers are removable, easy to clean and care for, and often feature a fully upholstered surface underneath.

For those with more traditional tastes, slipcovers offer a laid-back look without losing style or refinement. Soft lines, pleats, and skirts deliver a relaxed but well-bred attitude. More contemporary slipcover styling is trim and tailored with exposed wooden legs to emphasize the slipcovered effect. Many contemporary slipcovered styles even include sectionals, enjoying their own revival thanks to their versatility and comfort.

The new living room is enjoyed every day, rather than waiting for the next cocktail party or book club. Multi-tasking is the buzzword at home as in business, calling for a new breed of furniture including entertainment cabinets and home offices tucked away in armoires and other clever storage pieces.

Even so, when it is time to entertain, these rooms transform beautifully. Comfort is key; deep, downy cushions invite family and friends to relax and stay awhile. Soft tactile fabrics, such as velvet and chenille, create spaces that welcome company with an assured, dressed-for-success look that speaks of hospitality and good taste without being stiff or formal.

Today's entertainment centers feature space for everything from televisions to books to workspaces. This massive entertainment center/bookcase encloses a hidden desk and provides ample storage space for all of your home entertainment needs. Photo courtesy of Bassett Furniture.

This living room offers overstuffed luxury in contrasting floral patterns. Photo courtesy of Ashley Furniture.

Victorian elegance is evident in this comfortable living room. Photo courtesy of Highland House/Thomasville.

This traditional-style oak wall unit will provide for all of your living room's storage needs. Photo courtesy of Kimball Furniture.

The richness of mission style can be found in this living room, which features luxurious leather seating and sleek wooden tables. Photo courtesy of Living.com.

This living room setting is an unexpected mixture of styles and materials. Photo courtesy of Retrospect.

This comfortable living room is firmly rooted in country style, with a few contemporary touches to add variety. Photo courtesy of Living.com.

This patterned chair is a stately presence in this parlor. Photo courtesy of Lexington Furniture.

This mahogany lounge set features hand-chiseled framework. Photo courtesy of Zencraft.

This settee and chair, covered in soft, sumptuous velvet, create an intimate conversation area. Photo courtesy of Room & Board.

Transform your living room into a tropical paradise with these wicker pieces. Photo courtesy of Zencraft.

Slipcovered furnishings offer a laid-back look without losing style or refinement. Photo courtesy of Kozyhome.

If your taste is more pared-down, the return to natural simplicity is made for you. Natural fibers like linen, cotton and wool are highly popular for seating, windows, and rugs. A new palette of natural neutrals offers soft greens, along with shades of khaki, beige, taupe, and other tranquil tones to complement the easy lines of today's preferred seating styles. Zen-like accessories, such as candles, tabletop fountains and dried branches, add to the soothing ambiance.

It's been said lately that the living room is dead. And it is true that some people are opting for environments like media rooms, exercise rooms, home offices, or billiard parlors instead of traditional living rooms. But for the most part, today's living rooms do all their predecessors did and more; they have simply stopped being a trophy room outside the stream of actual daily life. Versatile, easy, and stylish, they are right in step with their owners and the times.

ITALIAN PAINTING
FRENCH PAINTING

Make yourself at home in this upscale living room set, featuring slipcovered sofas and eclectic accessories. Photo courtesy of Living.com.

This leather sofa has an antique appearance that lends presence to this home. Photo courtesy of Kozyhome.

An Arts & Crafts–style rocker and lamp create a comfortable reading corner. Photo courtesy of Kozyhome.

Urban sophistication abounds in this living room, which features streamlined sofas and rustic tables. Photo courtesy of Living.com.

This modern living room, featured in bright eggplant, has an easy, relaxed style, offering comfort combined with durability. Photo courtesy of Rooms to Go.

Combining contemporary styling with hot colors, this curvaceous living room is alluring, inviting and versatile. Photo courtesy of Rooms to Go.

This plush living room set is upholstered in a chic earth-tone chenille fabric and accented with abstract print toss pillows. Photo courtesy of Rooms to Go.

This contemporary living room offers a warm welcome to visitors. Unique accent chairs define the design, making this collection exciting. Photo courtesy of Rooms to Go.

An exercise in elegance, this living room provides comfort as well as timeless style. Photo courtesy of Rooms to Go.

This comfortable sectional, bursting with throw pillows, is ideal for entertaining. Photo courtesy of Rooms to Go.

This dapper leather chair, made of rich brown leather, is sure to reflect your impeccable taste. Photo courtesy of Kozyhome.

This modern sofa fuses chic design with sublime comfort, and is upholstered in velvety chenille. Photo courtesy of Kozyhome.

Tweed upholstery and traditional-style occasional tables produce a classic living room. Photo courtesy of Kozyhome.

Simply designed and well tailored, these sofas are covered in luxurious imported Italian top-grain black leather. Photo courtesy of Rooms to Go.

Classic design makes this mission-style door chest a pleasure to display in any room of your home. Photo courtesy of Kimball Furniture.

This dresser provides attractive storage space for hard-to-furnish areas like this hallway. Photo courtesy of Kimball Furniture.

This stately entertainment center anchors this living room and provides storage space for everything from home electronics to books. Photo courtesy of Guy Chaddock and Company.

Entertainment center. Photo courtesy of Pier 1 Imports.

Sleek, simple styling and welcome comfort make this living room set a perfect match for any home. Photo courtesy of Rooms to Go.

sofa gallery

(Clockwise, from top left:)

Classic tuxedo-style sofa. Photo courtesy of Councill Furniture.

Leather sofa. Photo courtesy of Henredon Furniture.

Rattan settee. Photo courtesy of Pier 1 Imports.

Sectional sofa. Photo courtesy of Room & Board.

Sectional sofa. Photo courtesy of Henredon Furniture.

Leather sofa. Photo courtesy of Kozyhome.

Savoy sofa. Photo courtesy of Councill Furniture.

(center:)

Tuxedo-style sofa. Photo courtesy of Henredon Furniture.

armchair gallery

(clockwise, from top left:)

Wicker, rattan and steel armchair. Photo courtesy of Pier 1 Imports.

Mission armchair. Photo courtesy of Barlow Tyrie.

Leather armchair. Photo courtesy of Kozyhome.

Mission rocking chair. Photo courtesy of Barlow Tyrie.

Rattan armchair. Photo courtesy of Pier 1 Imports.

Traditional leather armchair. Photo courtesy of Councill Furniture.

Giving Your Kitchen a Timeless Quality

by Bonnie Richardson
courtesy of ImproveNet.com

With good planning and careful attention to the selection of materials, you can develop a kitchen that will last a lifetime—one that will age gracefully and only become more comfortable over time. The best way to illustrate this is by answering the following questions.

I want to be sure I'm getting good value for my investment. What can I do to make sure my kitchen will stay current?

A kitchen that fits the character of the rest of the house will always be in style. That does not mean it has to have a period look, but its materials and finishes should complement the balance of the house. Traffic patterns, workspaces, lighting, and ventilation need to be carefully considered. If a kitchen functions well—if it's comfortable for just about any cook—it will be easy to update in the future.

Do some materials resist looking out of date better than others?

You can always rely on the beauty of natural materials. A variety of wood grains and finishes will remain current over time. Granite and other stone will provide quality surfaces that will complement many different styles. Stainless steel, tin, copper, and galvanized metal are also interesting materials that offer a lasting finish.

Mission serving table. Photo courtesy of Barlow Tyrie.

A traditional kitchen might include an elegant island like this one, which includes storage shelves underneath the workspace. Photo courtesy of Kimball Home.

Melding traditional materials with contemporary style, this dining room is an elegant spot for entertaining. Photo courtesy of Living.com.

Casual yet sophisticated, this dining set exudes old-world charm. Photo courtesy of Pottery Barn.

This Arts-and-Crafts-inspired counter makes a great kitchen island, work area, or breakfast nook. Photo courtesy of Room & Board.

Enjoy a leisurely breakfast or lunch in this charming farmhouse-style dining room. Photo courtesy of Living.com.

This spacious dining room, furnished in the mission style, is a prime dinner-party location. Photo courtesy of Living.com.

Simple and elegant dining in the kitchen is now possible, thanks to this compact dining set. Photo courtesy of Crate & Barrel.

Comfort and simplicity are key elements in this French country-style dining room. Photo courtesy of Living.com.

Contemporary style often features furnishings in bright, vibrant colors, as pictured in this dining ensemble. Photo courtesy of Kozyhome.

I like all the new trendy colors, but I worry about committing something as permanent as my kitchen to them.

If you know you like change, plan for it. Try cabinets that have a paint-grade finish, with a simple shape and solid structure. In five or six years you can repaint and install new hardware accessories and have a totally new look. Most appliances today have panel inserts that accommodate a face changing.

Color is an important element. Strong, bold hues can give the room vitality, but owners often tire of colors after a few years. The answer is not necessarily an all white or beige kitchen. Just restrict colors to paintable surfaces, fabrics, and accessories that can be easily changed.

Is there any rule of thumb regarding storage?

You can never go wrong by designing substantial storage into a kitchen. Walk-in pantries are always appreciated. Include a few outlets in the pantry at counter height, and you can turn one

Dining Armoire. Photo courtesy of Kimball Furniture.

shelf into an appliance counter. Good planning is important when it comes to storage. Often-used items need to be easily accessible, while seasonal serving pieces can be tucked away in a more remote location.

What can you do with a kitchen that looks like it's trapped in a time warp?

It is true that some things will come and go: trash compactors and harvest-gold and avocado appliances. Retrofitting those items is generally pretty simple if the balance of the kitchen works well. The space for the trash compactor can be redesigned for pull-out recycling bins, and most appliances can be replaced with little or no cabinet adjustment. However, if the refrigerator is located in the wrong place to begin with, it's still going to be in the wrong place no matter what color it is. And if the countertop is royal-blue laminate, it may be difficult to work into a new color palette.

This elegant buffet showcases elements of traditional Chinese design. Photo courtesy of Retrospect.

Tradition and style merge beautifully in this tasteful Arts & Crafts–style dining room. Photo courtesy of Furniture.com.

Country style is both casual and welcoming, as seen in this dining room. Photo courtesy of Furniture.com.

Sleek and smooth, this dining set is on the cutting edge of contemporary design. The gleaming satin nickel-finish frame, maple veneer table top, and swirl-patterned solid upholstery combine to make this a stylish dining group. Photo courtesy of Rooms to Go.

This dining collection is a perfect example of today's popular urban contemporary design. Clean maple veneers with inlaid accents are paired to create a dining room that is simply amazing. Photo courtesy of Rooms to Go.

Profile: Since graduating from Arizona State University in 1983 with a bachelor of architecture degree, Bonnie Richardson has worked for local architecture firms. She established her independent practice in 1987 and has also served for many years as a faculty associate in the College of Architecture and Environmental Design at ASU.

Dining Rooms: Spaces for Living and Entertaining

The dining room, along with the living room and kitchen, makes up the communal living area for your home and provides space for entertaining. Fortunately, the dining room is probably the easiest room in the house to decorate, since it has one specific function. Consider these points when preparing to furnish your dining room:

- ❖ What kind of dining room do you want? A small space for your family, a formal area for Thanksgiving dinners, or a casual, open area where guests can mingle? Consider your needs before purchasing your furnishings.

Dining table with lazy Susan. Photo courtesy of Barlow Tyrie.

❖ Start with selecting the dining table—it will be the room's main attraction, as well as the center of your design plan. Select chairs that will fit comfortably around the table.

❖ Once you've chosen the table and chairs, think about whether or not you need sidepieces. If you need display and storage space for china, silverware, and other accessories, a china hutch might come in handy. If you like to serve meals buffet style, a buffet might be appropriate.

❖ If you would like your dining room to have a more formal appearance, consider investing in a chandelier to hang above the center of the table. For a more casual approach, choose a less formal lighting fixture.

❖ Consider selecting a rug that will enhance your dining room's appearance. The rug should be large enough to fit the table as well as the chairs.

❖ Make sure you have enough space for guests to comfortably dine. You should allow 24 inches for each place setting, and at least that much space behind each chair (when someone is seated).

Mission dining table. Photo courtesy of Barlow Tyrie.

The delicate curves and classic proportions of this graceful dining set invite you to sit down in style. The balance of aged metal and cherry finish accents create a warm and inviting look. Photo courtesy of Rooms to Go.

This sideboard from Habersham has a warm, rich look that adds life to this room. Photo courtesy of Habersham Designs.

This dining room set adds a touch of elegance to this country setting. Photo courtesy of Bassett Furniture.

Casual elegance best describes this dining room. Crafted of pine solids and veneers, it features rich details like sturdy and stylish, turn-post legs, and a large extension table for seating many dinner guests. Slat back chairs offer a linear look, while upholstered seats are neutral to match any décor. Photo courtesy of Rooms to Go.

Bodega buffet. Photo courtesy of Mulholland Brothers.

Monaco dining chair. Photo courtesy of Barlow Tyrie.

Tessera dining table. Photo courtesy of Pier 1 Imports.

This Asian-inspired dining room setting lends elegance to a small dining area. Photo courtesy of Room & Board.

Inspired by mid-twentieth-century design, this sleek dining room set hits all the right notes. Photo courtesy of Room & Board.

Smooth lines and unique angles characterize this modern dining set. Photo courtesy of Furniture.com.

This modern-styled kitchen table set provides a fresh look for this kitchen. Photo courtesy of Room & Board.

Bedroom Decorating Tips

courtesy of WestpointStevens.com

At the start of the new millennium, the trend is toward a simpler, cleaner, less embellished look that goes hand in hand with furniture that is more sleek and pared-down. Jazz up your bedroom by incorporating these suggestions—and make your linen budget stretch as far as your imagination.

❖ A gorgeous new bedding ensemble can completely transform a lackluster bedroom. Luxurious texture and pattern will make your bed the focal point of the room, taking attention away from ordinary architecture or unappealing carpeting.

❖ Your first purchase should be a comforter. It's the starting point for your color scheme. If your comforter is reversible, you have more style and color options.

❖ Warm up a room and give it a feeling of intimacy by adding pillows or shams in colors that are complementary to one of the room's main colors.

❖ A duvet cover—a "pillowcase" for your comforter—can personalize a comforter by adding instant pattern and color to the bed. Just make sure that the cover's color is darker than the original comforter so that deep colors or bright patterns don't show through.

❖ Duvet covers can be changed to suit your mood or the season. Or you can display them all at once. For example, you could use one duvet that is lighter and more summery (like one made of seersucker) and another that is heavier and more wintry (like corduroy and velvet).

A bedroom designed in the country style is warm and inviting. Photo courtesy of Living.com.

This black iron bed is a cozy retreat from the world. Photo courtesy of Crate & Barrel.

This heirloom-style bed with handmade quilt reminds one of childhood summers spent at Grandma's house. Photo courtesy of Pottery Barn.

❖ Double-layer your bedskirts to achieve an abundant, more decorative look (and you'll be able to conceal things under your bed at the same time!) Just pin a second bedskirt over the first one, leaving four to six inches of the bottom skirt showing.

❖ Pillow shams are meant to be decorative. Keep two sets of pillows—one set on which to sleep and an extra set in your shams. Just think of the time you'll save by not having to pull your pillows out of the shams each night!

❖ When making your bed, you can place your pillows either in front of or behind your shams. Vary the positioning from time to time for a new look.

❖ Place heavier throw rugs, such as Oriental and needlepoint carpets, by your bedside and in heavily trafficked areas.

❖ Keep your comforter or spread turned down to show the pattern on its reverse side and to show off the colors of neatly tucked sheets.

Traditional dresser. Photo courtesy of Councill Furniture.

This exquisitely-designed bed is enhanced by comfortable linens and the elegant draperies hanging behind it. Photo courtesy of Living.com.

The bold, geometric lines of this bed add drama to this bedroom. Photo courtesy of Room & Board.

This casual bedroom suite melds the warm, welcoming tone of pine and cherry veneers with the strong statement of lacquered metal accents, creating a terrific lodge-style bedroom. Photo courtesy of Rooms to Go.

As fresh as a cool breeze, this country bedroom pairs a pine bed with bright white furnishings. Photo courtesy of Living.com.

The simple, masterfully crafted all-wood mission bedroom has been a favorite for generations. The look is timeless, and this bedroom set is a fine reproduction of classic early-twentieth-century American furniture styling. Photo courtesy of Rooms to Go.

This spectacular bedroom combines the casual air of honey pine with the richness of cherry wood veneers for an updated look. Dramatic pine lattice detailing is an eye-catching accent paired with the warm cherry woodwork. Photo courtesy of Rooms to Go.

This modern bedroom collection has a retro feel to it. Photo courtesy of Furniture.com.

Shaker style features simple furnishings with classic style, as seen in this bedroom. Photo courtesy of Furniture.com.

This tasteful dresser provides ample storage as well as a display area for accessories. Photo courtesy of Lexington Furniture.

Mactan-stone side table. Photo courtesy of Zencraft.

This Eastern-style bed is wrapped in leather. Photo courtesy of Zencraft.

Mahogany console set. Photo courtesy of Zencraft.

Natural wood finishes, sleek design, and sharp angles are characteristic of mission style, as seen in this bedroom. Photo courtesy of Kimball Furniture.

Offering the inviting warmth and elegance of French country, this bedroom features a beautiful washed pine finish, and has a wonderful rustic appeal. Details like wrought-iron scrollwork and accents bring to mind a country cabin or country-side villa. Photo courtesy of Rooms to Go.

This bedroom combines charm with modern design for a clean, unified look. Free of ornaments, the sleigh bed takes versatility and fashion to new heights. Photo courtesy of Rooms to Go.

With its abundance of pillows, this gracious French country-style bed exudes elegance. Photo courtesy of Highland House/Thomasville.

The sleek styling and mix of materials in this bed give it a refined look, referencing contemporary furniture design from the mid-twentieth century. Photo courtesy of Room & Board.

Exploding with pattern and color, this stylish bedroom set conjures up romantic images of plantation living. Photo courtesy of Waverly.

This massive yet stately bedroom set is a mighty presence in this bedroom. Photo courtesy of Ashley Furniture.

Curves are found all over this graceful bedroom set. Photo courtesy of Segusino/Marina's.

The urban contemporary styling of this superbly-crafted honey maple bedroom is an expression of classic new American design. The subtle curves, brushed steel hardware, and delicate spindles make this bedroom an ideal choice for any home. Photo courtesy of Rooms to Go.

This charming oak sleigh bed, accented with iron scroll detail, makes a dramatic addition to this bedroom. Photo courtesy of Kozyhome.

This sleigh bed has a honey colored finish with reddish undertones, making it a sleek addition to the bedroom. Photo courtesy of Kozyhome.

This sophisticated bed is made for city living. Photo courtesy of Mulholland Brothers.

This slat-headboard bed, made of hardwood and cherry veneers in a deep, dark finish, fuses classic design with contemporary style. Photo courtesy of Kozyhome.

A romantic scene is set in this tropical-flavored bedroom, complete with lush linens and island-friendly accessories. Photo courtesy of Kozyhome.

This roomy bathroom features privacy-friendly shades, as well as a number of other accessories that turn it into a comfortable retreat. Photo courtesy of Blinds2You.

Bathroom Design Basics

by Debra Sykes
excerpt courtesy of Kitchen-Bath.com

The bathroom is usually one of the smallest rooms in the house. But you can make the space look bigger with smart use of color and lines.

- ❖ For example, a bright-colored tub or toilet (like black or fire-engine red) next to white walls will have more visual weight and could overpower a small room. Exposed shelving, conversely, has less weight and makes the space seem bigger.

- ❖ Keep vertical lines to a minimum; they add height to a room. Horizontal lines (vanity tops, cabinets and moldings) visually expand the space.

- ❖ Light walls and floors make a room seem larger. Also, patterns made up of small elements give the impression of being farther away, an illusion that seems to extend the walls.

- ❖ Mirrors add length, depth and width. Consider an entire mirrored wall to double the size of the bathroom. Skylights, windows, and glass-block walls also add space.

An oversized bathtub next to a broad, sunny window—what could be more luxurious? Photo courtesy of Blinds2You.

Home Offices: A Growing Phenomenon

courtesy of Furniture.com

Planning a Home Office

Home offices are a growing phenomenon in the furniture world—and how could it be otherwise? Personal computers and laptops have changed our work habits, making a major impact on home planning.

People are using their home offices to run small businesses, manage personal finances, research purchases, or chart the family genealogy. They are creating the great American novel (or Website), doing homework, and emailing people they know.

Trend-spotter and marketing guru Faith Popcorn recently called the home "today's top choice for office space," noting the number of at-home workers is up 100% over the last five years. No wonder so many people are expanding their home offices!

About 42% of home offices have a dedicated room, but most people are carving office space out of rooms already performing another function. That means bedrooms, family and living rooms, and even kitchens and dining rooms. The operative word in such home offices is "home."

Others may need to place greater emphasis on the office aspect. These consumers need furniture that looks good and performs even better, with niches and designated areas for computer components, as well as storage for papers, books, software, and other office amenities.

Whatever category you fall in, it's a good idea to evaluate your real needs as you plan a home office. There are many handsome furniture options, but to create the best office for your home, you should also consider some of the following points:

This streamlined desk set, complete with computer and printer stands, makes working at home a pleasure. Photo courtesy of Crate & Barrel.

Your home office can be tucked neatly away into this armoire, which also provides plenty of storage space. Photo courtesy of Pottery Barn.

This office is casually elegant with its sleek desk and relaxed reading area. Photo courtesy of Room & Board.

Office armoire. Photo courtesy of Councill Furniture.

How much space do I actually have for an office?

Take a hard look at your office area, whether it's a whole room or a portion of one.

- Use a tape measure to delineate exactly how much space you actually have. People have a tendency to underestimate how much room a desk and chair actually require.
- Remember that electrical outlets and a phone jack must be near your desk. This may seem obvious, but such details can be overlooked when you're juggling space considerations.
- Do you need file cabinets, bookcases, or additional work surfaces . . . and did you plan enough space for them and for moving around the room?

Who will be using this space, and how?

This information affects not only the amount of workspace you need, but cost, maintenance, and cleaning issues. A computer workstation for children must be practical with a durable, easily cleaned surface. An adult's office in a home library or living area, on the other hand, can go upscale to be as handsome as it is practical.

If you need to keep lots of stuff organized (and who doesn't?), your home office should do that for you. While much of today's office

This desk is a unique blend of Eastern design and Western function. Photo courtesy of Room & Board.

This bookcase brings clean lines and sleek sophistication to this office. Photo courtesy of Crate & Barrel.

furniture has nooks, crannies, and niches for storing electronics and computer components, you still need to plan a bit.

❖ How much computer hardware and related equipment do you have? Measure everything you have to accommodate, so you can be sure your printer or tower will fit in the designated spaces.

❖ How much paper do you have to file? How many books, CDs, magazines, software boxes, and other items do you need to shelve? Do you need a bookcase or will a hutch top on your desk do the job?

❖ Where will you store printer paper and other bulk supplies?

Be realistic about your own work habits.

Is a desk adequate or do you need more work surface?

❖ Don't sacrifice your major work needs. If you need a drafting or work table, plan for it.

❖ An L-shaped desk and return provides lots of extra working surface. Returns are arrangements that use quite a lot of floor space, so you have to be sure about dimensions. For ordering purposes, you must know whether the return is to the right or left of the chair.

❖ Consider credenzas, modulars, and/or corner units as a way to create the configuration that's best for you. They can be amazingly adaptable, but once again, know the furniture's dimensions and how much space you really have.

This office features plenty of work space, and comes complete with a bookcase, work table, and armoire-style desk for your computer. Photo courtesy of Hooker Furniture.

For those who desire a more traditional office space, this vintage-style desk and chair is the perfect solution. Photo courtesy of Pottery Barn.

This office armoire is ideal for compact spaces, or for sharing living room or bedroom space. Photo courtesy of Kimball Furniture.

: desk recreates the tradition of the Arts & Crafts ·ement, and updates it with the unexpected use of natural steel. Photo courtesy of Room & Board.

If you have to carve a home office out of a room that's already being used for another function, be creative.

❖ Considering rearranging. Don't try to shoehorn everything into existing empty spaces, but start from scratch and consider all possible configurations.

❖ Keep an open mind about which room to use. Your first thought may not be the best solution for space, privacy, and neatness. Look at other rooms with a fresh eye.

❖ Be realistic about the way you work. If you're not the neat desk type, use as many options as possible to hide clutter and protect personal information. Arrange the room so the desk is not dominant. For an office in a kitchen, active family room, or children's room, seek furniture that's practical and easily cleaned.

❖ Consider using a decorative element like plants or folding screens to create a partial visual and psychological barrier between your office area and the rest of the room.

❖ Don't forget about self-contained office centers built into armoires. They can be a wonderfully compact way to house (and hide) a home office and are both attractive and highly compatible with other home furnishings.

Office armoire. Photo courtesy of Mulholland Brothers.

This computer desk maximizes your space by taking advantage of a room's corner. Photo courtesy of Ashley Furniture.

Featuring a more delicate look, this graceful desk with iron scrolling will add beauty to your home office. Photo courtesy of Hooker Furniture.

With ample storage space and a separate work table, this desk is certain to suit all of your office needs. Photo courtesy of Stanley Furniture.

This unique baker's-rack desk is especially well-suited for the kitchen or living room. Photo courtesy of Hooker Furniture.

finding space in your place

One thing that many apartments and first homes have in common is a lack of space. Even in larger homes, there always seem to be a couple of areas where you just don't have enough room. For the space-challenged, here are a few ideas to help you cope:

- ❖ Color plays an important part in how spacious a room feels. Light, neutral colors create the illusion of space, as do monochromatic color schemes.
- ❖ Look for furnishings made of open-weave materials like wicker or rattan.

This sofa converts to a comfortable twin-sized bed, allowing you or a guest to sleep in luxury. Photo courtesy of Bassett Furniture.

- Furnishings raised off the ground (such as end tables with legs) will also help open up the room.
- Consider incorporating items that serve multiple purposes: a cedar chest that doubles as a coffee table, futons or sleeper sofas, or breakfast nooks that double as food-preparation areas.
- Take advantage of your wall space—put up shelves to store more of your stuff, and free up some floor space at the same time.
- Don't feel like you have to display every knickknack you own at the same time.
- Group your collections together so they'll look more organized, and rotate them every so often. Not only will you have more space, you'll also be able to give your room a fresh look.

This marble-topped kitchen counter-style table, shown with two stools, doubles as a breakfast nook and an extra food-preparation area—perfect for homes with small kitchens or dining areas. Photo courtesy of Pottery Barn.

Sunny yellow walls add a cheerful spirit to this bedroom. Photo courtesy of Stanley Furniture.

rooms with a view: walls and windows

Don't overlook the most important details of your house—the walls and windows. For many people, these details are an afterthought, and so they settle for plain white walls and ordinary window blinds. But nothing can improve the appearance of your home more than painting the walls or changing the window coverings. In fact, painting or wallpapering the walls is the easiest (and the cheapest!) thing you can do if you want to freshen up a room's appearance. Window coverings can also be quite economical and, in some cases, easily made—even by those who can't even sew on a button.

Many people are wary of tackling walls and windows themselves, preferring to leave them to professionals. But it's easier than you think, especially if you keep in mind a few important guidelines. Professionals from Designviews.com and IHome.com explore the many options for walls and windows.

Some Pointers for Painters

courtesy of Designviews.com

Do you select wall color first or last? Traditional decorating advice says to decorate a room from the outside in. In other words, select your wall color first. For those creating their rooms over time, though, wall color is often the one thing that can pull it all together in the end.

How do you tell which color is right?

Start with paint chips—for instance, bring home several shades of blue even if they don't look close. What looks awful at the paint store may look great at home. Keep narrowing until you've got it down to two or three shades or colors. Then get a quart of all the contenders and have fun! Always start by painting a big (at least 3' x 3') swatch of color on the wall and live with it for a few days. Don't try all the colors at once. Move furniture up against the color. How does it look in the morning, late afternoon, after dark? How does it fit the other elements in the room? You'll know when it feels right.

How much paint do you need?

Several websites boast easy-to-use paint calculators. Benjamin Moore (www.benjaminmoore.com) has a good one, along with answers to many painting dilemmas and a guide for selecting specific paints for each project. Ace Hardware (www.acehardware.com) also has a good paint estimator, as does Home Depot (www.homedepot.com).

Color trend predictions for the next decade: blue, both medium and dark; red, peaches, and terra-cottas, grays, and techno-brights.

Twenty-one Ways to Spice Up Your Walls

courtesy of Designviews.com

Old plates—Moroccan, Mexican, any plates with color, texture, and character.

Masks—ceremonial masks from any culture.

Horns or antlers—give the deer and elk a rest, and try something exotic.

Shallow round baskets—Indian baskets with interesting geometric patterns.

Machine parts and gears—clean 'em up and showcase together in one big dramatic display.

Old tools—especially gardening tools with great patina; again, group them for maximum effect.

Numbers or letters—vintage-look metal and wood letters and numbers inspired by old signs make bold groupings.

Straw hats—one will look ordinary, but a dozen will have impact.

Empty picture frames—lean some big ones against the wall or over the fireplace.

A narrow shelf—create an ever-changing scene by rotating objects on a narrow shelf.

Rows of vintage knobs—place them in a line down a hall or in a laundry room. Use them for hanging umbrellas or straw bags.

Game boards—many old ones have rich colors and patterns.

Old canes—display a row of them evenly spaced.

Mossy green walls set off this cupboard and evoke country charm. Photo courtesy of Pulaski Furniture.

iris blue with golden rattan
citron with powder blue
chartreuse with slate blue
dark peach with dark blue
terra-cotta with turquoise
terra-cotta with celadon
tomato with cream
tangerine with tangy light green
pale blue with stone

great color combos

cobalt with blond

terra-cotta with brick red

saffron with warm wood

Hula skirts—the real raffia ones, not the plastic imitations. Get them from party supply stores. Let them hang from the center point only, like a giant raffia tassel.

Rows of hooks—hang them high so the objects they display are at eye level.

Chalkboards—in sets of three—totally practical for kitchens, home offices, and garages. Be bold and use them in unexpected places, like a dining room or bedroom. Keep lots of colored chalk handy.

Bulletin boards—Another clever "create your own" art idea—paint all the frames the same color.

Cane fishing poles—group them in corners, leaning against the wall.

Spears—or any other ceremonial weapons.

Anything funky—if it has personality and you love it, figure out a way to hang it up. One daring soul covered a chair in a fabric from a vintage skirt and hung the matching bra top over the chair.

Lining a wall with floor-to-ceiling bookshelves will create a three-dimensional showcase for everything from books to framed photographs to vases. Photo: Trisha Ison.

The corner windows in this bedroom are enhanced with wide-slat blinds and tab-top curtains. Photo courtesy of Blinds2You.

Screens can add textural variety to any room, as well as create privacy or block unwelcome sunlight from a window. Photo courtesy of Waverly.

White vertical blinds stretch across this room, creating a streamlined look. Photo courtesy of Blinds2You.

A valance hangs over three narrow kitchen windows, each covered by mini-blinds. Photo courtesy of Blinds2You.

A textured blue fabric shade, paired with a window scarf, lends a casual elegance to this living room. Photo courtesy of Blinds2You.

Window Dressing

excerpt courtesy of IHome.com

Window treatments are often the most overlooked and misunderstood components of a home's décor. In fact, they are an integral part of setting the tone of a room or bringing a look together. Window coverings can be purely functional and subtle, simply serving to regulate light and privacy, or they can make an opulent statement, directing the eye towards the window or providing an elegant frame for the view outdoors. In any case, they are essential parts of your décor and should be taken into consideration when designing a home.

A well-dressed window can be a reflection of your personal taste, but you'll also need to take into account your lifestyle and environment. If you live in a colder climate, window treatments can serve as insulation. They can also block out noise and the glare of sunlight that might harm your artwork and furnishings. If you have a hectic lifestyle, it is wise to choose durable, easy-to-care-for fabrics. Save heavy elaborate drapes for less frequently used rooms. The length of the panels is also a factor to consider. Floor-to-ceiling treatments can add height to a room, but beware of little children and playful pets that may be tempted by all that fabric. Choosing the appropriate window hardware is also important. They can be simple and understated or add to the drama of the window with metal flourishes and exotic shapes.

no cash? no worries!

If you're reading this book, perhaps you've just paid your first and last months' rent (and deposit) on your new place, or spent even more money on a down payment. Needless to say, you're broke! But never fear—that doesn't mean you have to spend the rest of your life in an empty house. These creative ideas will help you to furnish and spruce up your place in no time.

❖ **Work with what you've got.** If all you have is an ugly brown sofa from your Aunt Myrtle—well, at least that's a start. If you're crafty, you could sew slipcovers for the sofa. If you're not, buy some flat sheets and tuck away, then add a few throw pillows. You'll be surprised at the improvement!

❖ **Get creative.** See those sheets you just used to create a sofa slipcover? Those same sheets could be used to make curtains, valances, tablecloths—even a canvas for a wall mural! Keep your eyes open for everyday objects that can be transformed into home décor: that old calendar might be full of potential wall art, and wine bottles make for great candleholders or bud vases.

❖ **Stay open-minded.** Chances are, you won't find the perfect sofa or table on your bargain-basement budget. But wood and metal can be repainted, and ugly fabric replaced or covered if necessary. Don't forget to consider alternate uses for objects—maybe that weird-shaped bookcase would make a great headboard.

❖ **Beg, borrow (but don't steal!)** Let your friends and family know that you're on the prowl for new furnishings. You can often find the best stuff this way, especially if you're willing to clean out someone's basement to get it.

❖ **Embrace the freedom of nature.** When it comes to free stuff, you can't beat Mother Nature! Venture outdoors to gather a few flowers from the yard, or perhaps a tree branch with its autumn leaves still attached. Gather up pebbles or pinecones and display them in an earthenware bowl. Just remember to ask the neighbors before chopping branches off their prized rosebushes.

Create your own canopy inexpensively by draping sheer material over a bed frame. Photo: Trisha Ison.

The current trend in window treatments seems to be towards subtle sleek panels and drapes that combine functionality and style. Achieve an airy look with the use of sheer panels and fabric scarves. The clean silhouette of white cotton makes a graceful statement in any room, and delicate yet durable lace is fashionable in any environment. Velvet drapes are good for those seeking privacy, and their lush and romantic feel make them ideal for the bedroom. Take your furnishings into account when choosing colors and fabrics. You want your windows to enhance the décor, not compete for attention. Examine your windows from all angles. Think about how your window treatments will look closed and open, and how they appear from the outside as well.

The key to decorating your windows is keeping in mind what length and type of treatment is suited to your window's size and shape. Here's a short list of basic window vocabulary to get you started:

Curtain: Usually unlined, a curtain is a panel of hemmed fabric hung from a rod at the top of a window. Panels can be floor length or end at the windowsill.

Finial: A decorative piece of metal attached to the ends of drapery rods.

Lining: Fabric used as a backing for drapery panels. Linings can provide body and fullness, light control, and privacy.

Rod Pocket Curtains: The most common window treatment. A stitched pocket at the top of the curtain is gathered or shirred onto a curtain rod.

Sheer: A drapery panel made of sheer or translucent fabric, sometimes used underneath an outer drapery or layered for a unique look.

Tab-Top Curtains: Drapes that hang from fabric bands into which a decorative curtain rod is inserted.

Tiebacks: Fabric bands that shape the curtain or drape and hold them back from the window.

Valance: A window treatment that covers the top of the window and the drapery hardware. A valance is made of matching or contrasting fabric and gathered over a curtain rod.

Window Scarf: A long, decorative piece of fabric casually draped over a pole or rod at the top of a window like a valance. The center is gently pulled down to create a soft curve. They are often used in addition to curtains or alone over blinds and shades.

Large windows, such as the arched living room windows shown here, are easily covered with vertical blinds. Photo courtesy of Blinds2You.

An elegantly patterned rug defines the space in this uniquely furnished home office. Photo courtesy of Bombay Company.

common ground: all about floors

You walk all over them—now it's time to give a little attention to that space under your feet, otherwise known as the floor. Designer Arlene Claiborne suggests beginning any room design with the floor, since it is the largest expanse of space in the room (along with the ceiling.) Should you choose carpeting, tile, laminate, or hardwood flooring? Do you need throw rugs? Choosing the floor that will give years of performance and enrich the charm of your rooms can be difficult if you don't understand your floor-covering options. This advice from FloorFacts.com and BeHome.com will help you get it right.

Flooring 101 Overview

courtesy of FloorFacts.com

Choosing the right floor . . .

This guide is meant to help you explore your floor-covering options, as well as to give you a better understanding of what to look for in a particular type of floor. Let's face it, buying a new floor can be a perplexing job. The following information will give you more confidence when shopping for flooring and make your experience a more pleasurable one.

For information about a specific product or for information about installing a specific floor, you should always refer to the manufacturer's written documents. Use this information as a basic guide to help you better understand how to choose the best floor for your specific needs.

Laminate Flooring: Exceptional Durability

Do you want the beautiful appearance of a real hardwood floor but with exceptional performance that will hold up from the wear and tear of children, pets, and spills? This question is in the minds of many American homeowners when shopping for a new floor. The answer many flooring shoppers have found is choosing one of the many laminate floors. These floors are similar in construction to the Formica kitchen counter tops but with some added performance features. All laminate floors have good performance characteristics and are often confused with real hardwood floors. Even though these floors resemble real wood floors, they are not wood.

Laminate floors offer many benefits for homeowners, including:

- Exceptional durability
- Easy-to-clean surface
- Superior stain and fade resistance
- Can be installed over many different types of subfloors
- Great impact and indentation resistance
- Exceptional realism at affordable costs
- Easy to replace later on if desired.

Hardwood Floors Overview: Natural Beauty

The elegant look of a hardwood floor can add warmth and character to any room in a home. The natural characteristics of wood add depth and a visual appearance that many other types of floors try to duplicate. As the consumer demand for hardwood floors has grown, so has the manufacturer's ability to produce better quality finishes and superior construction techniques. With these advancements, wood floors can now be installed throughout the home and over a wide variety of subfloors. Today, homeowners looking to use wood floors have the option of purchasing three different types of wood flooring: 3/4" solid wood floors, engineered plank floors, or long-strip plank floors. Although the end results may look the same, there are distinct advantages for using each type in different situations.

Once installed, it is extremely difficult to tell the difference between a solid-wood floor and the other wood floors. Both the engineered and the longstrip floors have thin layers of wood that are glued together. By gluing the plies together, you get better dimensional stability within the plank itself, which allows these floors to be used on job sites that have a higher percentage of moisture content than normal. This includes

Hardwood floors offer simple, understated support for a chair that is both elegant and comfortable. Photo courtesy of Highland House/Thomasville.

The vivid colors and geometric patterns in this rug will add a contemporary flair to your floor. Photo courtesy of Room & Board.

basements and over concrete slabs where solid-wood floors are considered off limits.

Another choice you have is whether to go with a pre-finished wood floor, or an unfinished wood floor. The pre-finished floors offer a wider variety of wood species and saves hours of labor and cleanup, while the unfinished wood floors allow you to have a custom job-site finish and the chance to level the surface of the entire floor after it has been installed. You also get an extended factory finish warranty with pre-finished floors, but not with most job-site finishes.

Vinyl Flooring: Floors with Style

Homeowners today are looking for more fashionable choices in their flooring selections. No other floor-covering category offers the selection, styling, and ease of maintenance as a vinyl floor. Thanks to some great advancements in styling and technology, vinyl floors have been changed forever. For example, the Mannington NatureForm Collections incorporate a unique manufacturing process, producing flooring that resembles the look and textures of real ceramic, stone and wood grain patterns. These amazing replicas have such incredible realism it is difficult for most people to tell whether it's the real thing or not.

Ceramic Tile: Timeless and Elegant

Ceramic tile has been around for centuries, and with today's technology, manufacturers have created new design and application possibilities that were not available a decade ago. If you have never used ceramic tile before, you will be amazed at the wide selection of colors, sizes, shapes, and new textures that are available.

Ceramic tile is a natural product made up of clay, a number of other naturally-occurring minerals, and water. Glazed ceramic tile has a ceramic coating applied to the tile body, which gives the tile its color and finish. Glazed ceramic tile is the most natural choice for your interior floors and walls. It is also:

- ❖ Durable—a properly installed ceramic tile will outperform and outlast nearly any other floor-covering product created for the same application.
- ❖ Easy care—glazed ceramic tile resists stains, odors, and dirt and can be cleaned up with a damp mop or sponge or common household cleaners such as Mr. Clean, Top Job or Spic and Span.
- ❖ Scratch resistant—Grade III and Grade IV glazed ceramic tiles are extremely resistant to scratching and you never have to worry about a cut or tear like you do with some other types of floors.
- ❖ Environmentally friendly—ceramic tile is manufactured using natural materials and does not retain odors, allergens, or bacteria.
- ❖ Beautiful and Versatile—modern ceramic manufacturing technology has created virtually an unlimited number of colors, sizes, styles, shapes, and textures that will add rich beauty and character to any room décor.
- ❖ Fire Resistant—ceramic tile doesn't burn nor emit toxic fumes. A lighted cigarette, when dropped on the floor, even if allowed to sit, will not do any damage to ceramic tile. Even hot kitchen pans or skillets will not scorch or melt the surface of glazed ceramic tile.

Collection of Kashimar rugs. Photo courtesy of Couristan.

- ❖ Water Resistant—most glazed ceramic tile has a dense body that permits little or no accumulation of moisture. This means spills from common liquids found in a kitchen are not a big concern.

Ceramic tile is a practical, functional choice for your floor, walls, or countertops, one that offers you a unique opportunity for self-expression because of its beauty, versatility, and design potential.

Carpet: Warmth and Comfort Underfoot

There is no doubt that carpet offers homeowners more warmth and softness, and is much quieter than any other floor covering. Today's carpet styles, colors, and textures blend well with any home décor and with a variety of other flooring products. From traditional to country to formal styles, you can always find a carpet that will enrich any interior setting and give you years of performance.

Listed below are a few advantages to using carpeting in your home:

- ❖ Carpet adds warmth and is soft underfoot and easier on children's knees.
- ❖ It is much quieter than hard-surfaced floors.
- ❖ It comes in a wide variety of color tones and hues.
- ❖ Carpet is easy to decorate with and offers many solid color tones for rooms with patterned wall coverings.
- ❖ Carpet can hide many subfloor irregularities that would not be permitted with hard-surfaced floors.
- ❖ It can go over a variety of substrates and on all grade levels, even concrete slabs in basements.
- ❖ Carpet is economical and the installation costs are much less than some of the hard surface products.

This dining room is defined by a cream-colored rug, which sets a casual tone for the tasteful dining set. Photo courtesy of Ashley Furniture.

Tips for Selecting a Rug

courtesy of BeHome.com

❖ There are faster ways to make a buck than by buying a rug and hoping its value increases. You should buy a rug because you like it (then you can pass it on to your kids).

❖ Measure the size of the room and decide how much of the floor you want underneath to be exposed. For example, if you're considering placing a rug underneath a dining room table, make sure it fits the entire set. The chairs should sit on the rug, not hang off the edges. A good rule of thumb: The rug should be two feet larger all around the table to accommodate chairs. Keep in mind that machine-woven rugs have approximate dimensions. For example, a 9' x 12' rug may actually be more like 8'6" x 10'10". Each machine-woven rug is different.

❖ If a rug defines a living space, make sure all the furniture in the room fits on it (often an 8' x 10' or larger). If a rug is to define a conversation area, it should be placed in front of the furniture, usually placed under a cocktail table (often a 5' x 8' or 6' x 9' is used).

❖ For high-traffic areas, choose a rug for its durability. A handmade hooked rug or a delicate antique, for example, may not be the best option. And don't be fooled into thinking that synthetics are more durable than wool. Wool is strong, resilient, naturally soil-resistant, and easy to clean. A good-quality wool rug will last thirty years or more.

❖ If your sofa has a very busy or intricate pattern, pick a rug with an open field in a contrasting color to set it off.

❖ Regular vacuuming and spot cleaning is fine for most rugs. For fine antiques or a particularly delicate rug, arrange for periodic cleaning by professional rug cleaners.

❖ Rug underlay, or no-slip padding, can prolong a rug's life (and yours, too—without an underlay, your rug might take you for a skate across your wood floor).

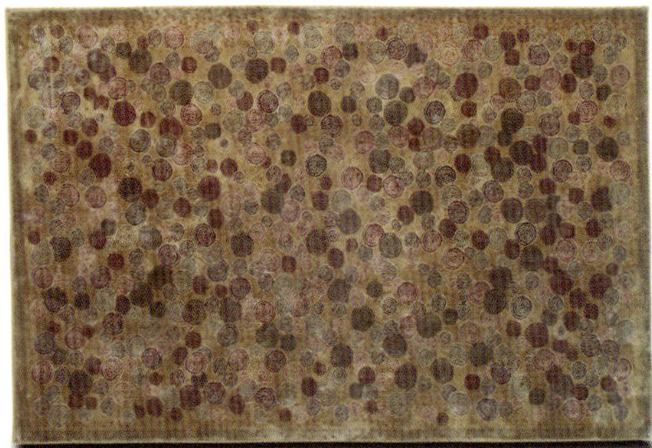

Monterre rug. Photo courtesy of Pier 1 Imports.

Sierra Design rug from Couristan's Mirage Collection. Photo courtesy of Couristan.

Paparazzi/Golden Sunburst rug from Couristan's Confetti Collection. Photo courtesy of Couristan.

living in a box: dealing with apartment restrictions

Feeling like a guest in your own home? You probably live in an apartment and feel like you can't make any changes to it. The good news is that many apartment managers will allow you to make minor changes to your apartment. Read on for some tips.

- Before signing your lease, ask your landlord what changes can be made to the apartment. Some apartment managers are more flexible if you're signing a long-term lease or moving into an older building. If you have the expertise, some landlords will even allow you to make upgrades to the apartment while knocking a few dollars off your rent.
- Always check with the landlord before making any changes to your apartment, even painting the walls. Most landlords won't stop you from painting walls or changing the light fixtures, as long as you restore the apartment to its original condition by the time you move out.
- If you are allowed to paint, stick to light, neutral tones—it will make repainting much easier. If you want to go with darker or brighter colors, keep in mind that you'll need to use a primer like Kilz before repainting the walls white.
- Even if you can't make changes to the apartment itself, don't sweat it. Adding throw or area rugs to the floor, hanging up pictures, mirrors, or tapestries, and draping curtains over the standard apartment-style blinds and shades will go a long way towards making your apartment feel like home.

Tarsus/Plum rug from Couristan's Turkomen collection. Photo courtesy of Couristan.

Eclipse/Golden Yellow rug from Couristan's Metropolis collection. Photo courtesy of Couristan.

Baku/beige rug from Couristan's Renaissance Series. Photo courtesy of Couristan.

Simya/Rose/Black rug from Couristan's Shalimar Collection. Photo courtesy of Couristan.

A modern-style lamp provides a bit of retro flair to this living room. Photo courtesy of Room & Board.

CHAPTER 7

shine on: what's new in lighting?

Lighting is both an accessory and a necessity, and while the singular beauty of light is worth celebrating, the fixtures that lightbulbs sit in are what add drama and interest to our homes. What kind of lighting will you need for your home? A home office may require task lighting such as a reading light over a desk, while decorative lighting will highlight accessories in your living room. The following advice (courtesy of Furniture.com) will help you begin answering this question for your home.

This sleek lamp features a sandcast aluminum base and white polycarbonate shade. Photo courtesy of Lighting Store USA.

Now is a great time for the colors silver and blue; paired on a lamp, these colors promise an instant best-seller. A sleek brushed-nickel base topped with a frosted cobalt shade is a fun way to add low-tech punch to high-tech décor. Blue lava lamps provide retro cool, and silver mesh and punched-out metals keep art deco up to the minute and kicking. Antique pewter, polished brass, nickel, and aluminum are the metals of the moment, turning ordinary fixtures into sculptures with sophistication and charm.

Ebonized woods, alabaster, and polycarbonate (an impact-resistant thermoplastic that's easily molded when hot) are popular materials currently sharing the spotlight. Lampshades are fashioned in just about everything, including parchment, linen, silk, leather, and even thin sheets of translucent wood. Glass shades draw inspiration from Depression glass (tinted glassware machine-produced during the 1930s), as well as Tiffany-style stained glass. Handblown forms bring sinuous shapes onto the scene, while color-treated glass transforms lampshades into artwork.

Illuminated occasional tables are blurring the lines between table and lamp, and foot-operated switches are giving new meaning to fumbling for the light. Manufacturers, catching onto the popularity of hardware store clamp-lights, are adding clamp options to even the priciest fixtures. Designs like protruding 3-D squiggles, dots, and ripples add humor to lights large and small. Curvaceous ladylike lamps are strutting their stuff, complete with teardrop pulls for a well-coifed look.

Nature is illuminated in fixtures of bamboo and stone, while painterly lampshades depicting grasses and Chinese characters calm even the harshest décors. Rectangular block pedestal table lamps have returned from the 1930s and are especially nice with white or natural linen lampshades. Frank Lloyd Wright inspirations include geometric motifs and the delicate-but-sturdy joinery typical of his work. A return to natural materials used in simple utilitarian designs recall the Arts and Crafts movement and mission ideals.

Permanent fixtures, such as sconces, pendants, and track lighting, are either hold-nothing-back whimsical or whisper-soft elegant. The opaque glow of sandblasted glass cooled with metal accents is a popular wall-fixture look. Cable tracks have returned from Victorian times and track-lighting fixtures are available in every color from apricot to light blue. Slim rails that can be hand-bent into loops turn dark ceilings into brilliant light shows, and fiber optics use pinpoints of light to create cosmic starfields on ceilings both inside and out. The latest buzz is silencing fluorescents: new designs are compact, flicker-proof, and have an impressive 10,000-hour life span.

Whether dressed up, barely there, or completely exposed, good lighting design today is always energy-efficient. Increased variety and lower costs have closed the gap between available styles and current trends, making lighting fixtures one of the most effective and dramatic ways to accessorize a room. When choosing lighting, always have a master plan and layer ambient, task, information, and decorative light.

A chandelier is the perfect finishing touch for this country dining room. Photo courtesy of Bassett Furniture.

the four types of light

Ambient lighting, also known as general or background lighting, is the light by which we see. It's a direct substitute or supplement for natural light and is supplied by table lamps and torchieres that reflect light off the ceiling or wall sconces, washing the wall with light.

Task lighting is for a specific activity or purpose and is usually directional and local. For example, a reading lamp angled over a desk or a downlight over the kitchen sink are both sources of task lighting.

Information lighting enables us to find our way in the dark. Sources include path lights along a walkway, an illuminated doorbell, and the light inside the refrigerator.

Decorative lighting, also called accent lighting, is discreet low-level light that is used to call attention to artwork, sculptures and architectural details. Recessed ceiling lights used to spotlight paintings and small lights in display cabinets are examples of decorative lighting.

This lamp, inspired by vintage luggage, illuminates a desktop. Photo courtesy of Bombay Company.

This whimsical floor lamp includes an umbrella shade and a nickel-finish stand and base. Photo courtesy of Lighting Store USA.

secondhand chic

The Joys of Thrift Shopping

So you're finally got a place of your own—but after coughing up all the cash just to get into it, chances are you probably don't have a lot of money left over. Maybe you've already purchased your major furnishings and just need to fill in the blanks with some cool accessories, or maybe you're starting from scratch. Either way, the cheapest way to add some character to your home or apartment is to hit the secondhand circuit—flea markets, estate sales, thrift stores, online auctions, and garage/yard sales.

Buying secondhand can be a time-consuming and frustrating process, but when you find the perfect couch for fifty dollars, it can also become an irresistible pleasure. And with a little creativity, patience, and a sense of your own style, you're guaranteed to end up with a unique-looking pad that your friends and neighbors will envy.

For the uninitiated, here are a few tips to keep in mind on your shopping journeys:

Flea Markets:

- ❖ The most appealing thing about flea markets is the huge selection of merchandise available from so many sellers. Of course, that can also be the least appealing aspect of flea-market shopping. If you go, be prepared to spend a lot of time sifting through the dross to unearth gold.
- ❖ If you're shopping for antiques or vintage items, do your research ahead of time. Make sure you know how much the items are going for in the marketplace—you'll avoid getting ripped off, and you'll be able to enjoy finding bargains all the more.

Estate Sales:

- ❖ If you're looking for higher-quality furniture and are willing to spend a little more, shop at estate sales. These are generally held after a person has died, and the family is trying to get rid of the contents of the deceased's home. Estate sales don't offer the cheapest prices, but you're almost sure to get great value for your money, since most of the items are usually in excellent condition. Browse the classified ads in the newspaper for estate-sale listings.

These mission-style table lamps from the Frank Lloyd Wright Collection are the ultimate in simplicity and design perfection. Photo courtesy of Lighting Store USA.

Thrift Stores:

- Shop at charity-affiliated thrift shops like Goodwill or Salvation Army for the best deals.
- Keep an open mind. Maybe that brown chair would look great with a slip-cover, or that kitchen table could be repainted to match your chairs.
- Be patient. If you don't find what you're looking for on your first visit, keep checking back every week for new additions. Talk to the store's employees and find out what days they do most of their restocking.

Online Auctions:

- Online auction sites like Ebay and Amazon.com Auctions are irresistible, as they offer an infinite number of items to choose from. However, buyers should exercise caution when making purchases online. Make sure that the seller offers a money-back guarantee on the item. Look to see if other buyers have rated the seller—if there have been any complaints, steer clear of the seller. Finally, be sure to calculate the shipping charges: this hidden cost can sometimes drive up the price enough that it is not worth the purchase.

Garage & Yard Sales:

- Do your homework. Check the papers ahead of time to find out where sales will be.
- Set that alarm clock—you'll want to start shopping early for the best selection.
- Carry cash. Most sellers don't like to accept personal checks.
- Don't be afraid to bargain with sellers.

Antique lamps, vintage luggage pieces, and well-worn leather armchairs are a few of the treasures that await secondhand shoppers. Photo: Trisha Ison.

The Frank Lloyd Wright Collection includes this mission-style table lantern with colored iridescent glass and a solid polished brass base. Photo courtesy of Lighting Store USA.

Mission-style lantern sconce from the Frank Lloyd Wright Collection. Photo courtesy of Lighting Store USA.

(left and right) These cherry wood lamps from the Frank Lloyd Wright Collection were designed with open, rectangular boxes. Photos courtesy of Lighting Store USA.

This green sconce is ideal for a hallway, stairway, or other area where discreet ambient lighting is desired. Photo courtesy of Lighting Store USA.

Retailers – Home Furnishings & Accessories

Abizaks (www.abizaks.com)

Offering the best in contemporary home furnishings, Abizaks features some of the most unusual, creative, and affordable furnishings you'll ever see.

Annise (www.annise.com)

A shop that embodies stylish living, infusing luxurious materials from exotic places with simple and elegant designs to create a unique and truly "Zensual" experience.

Ballard Designs (www.ballarddesigns.com)

Founded in 1983, Ballard Designs is one of the premier mail-order sources for fine home furnishings and accents.

Beaver Home (www.beaverhome.com)

Offers high-quality furnishings, flooring, cabinets, and other items for the home at low prices.

Bed Bath & Beyond (www.bedbathandbeyond.com)

Chain of superstores offering bed linens, bath accessories and kitchen textiles, as well as cookware, dinnerware, glassware and basic housewares.

BeHOME (www.behome.com)

A pioneering marketer of home furnishings on the Internet, Benchmark BeHOME harmonizes over thirty years of experience in home furnishings with the capabilities of the Internet to bring their customers the best values on the highest quality furniture.

resource guide

Bloomingdale's (www.bloomingdales.com)
The world-renowned department store offers many of their upscale home accessories and a limited amount of furniture online.

The Bombay Company (www.bombayco.com)
With over 400 stores in North America, the Bombay Company is one of the largest furniture chains around. The style and tone of Bombay reflects a sophisticated look featuring classic and traditional furniture, as well as coordinating accessories and wall décor.

Calico Corners (www.calicocorners.com)
Helping your style come to life with fabrics and furniture to inspire you and the custom services to get the job done.

Chiasso (www.chiasso.com)
From the sensationally mod to the fabulously fun, Chiasso offers modern products that look great, work well, and lift the spirit.

Circa 50 (www.circa50.com)
Offering modern-style furnishings, lighting, and accessories.

The Company Store (www.thecompanystore.com)
Shop online for their bath and bedding products, as well as for home furnishings and accessories.

Cosmopolitan Home (www.cosmopolitanhome.com)
A one-stop shop for home accessories and furniture.

Cost Plus World Market (www.costplus.com)
A complete value retailing resource which provides simple yet unique solutions for every entertaining and decorating need.

Crate & Barrel (www.crateandbarrel.com)
Founded in 1962, Crate & Barrel is one of the most respected retailers of fine housewares and furniture.

Decorate Today (www.decoratetoday.com)
Offering quality name-brand blinds and wallpaper, plus top quality rugs, lighting fixtures, and wall art. They offer live assistance from decorating experts, as well as helpful hints for decorating.

Design Centro Italia (www.italydesign.com)
Direct importers of high-style modern Italian furniture from over fifty of Italy's leading manufacturers.

Design Within Reach (www.dwr.com)
Offers easy access to well-designed furniture, frequently found only in designer showrooms, which can be shipped to you in a week.

Domestications (www.domestications.com)
A leader in home fashions, offering the latest in bedding, rugs, window coverings, dinnerware and more.

Down East Outfitters (www.downeastoutfitters.com)
Outlet stores that offer a broad selection of top-quality home furnishings at 50 percent off the name-brand prices.

Drexel Heritage (www.drexelheritage.com)
Visit their Drexel Heritage, Lillian August, and Drexel Studio collections online and locate a dealer in your area.

Eddie Bauer Home (www.eddiebauer.com)
Bringing the casual, relaxed comfort of Eddie Bauer sportswear to the bed and bath is the philosophy behind the collection of furnishings and décor from Eddie Bauer Home.

Ethan Allen (www.ethanallen.com)
Browse their furniture collections online, shop for accents and textiles, and find a retail location near you.

EzSHOP.com (www.ezshop.com)
Internet superstore, offering a variety of home décor and furnishings to choose from.

Frontera (www.frontera.com)
Originally founded as a retailer and mail-order catalog of high quality, Frontera offers traditionally made furniture, including its signature "Brazos River Rocker."

Frontgate (www.frontgate.com)
First established as a mail-order company, Frontgate offers functional, high-quality products for the entire home environment, both indoors and out.

Full Upright Position (www.f-u-p.com)
The source for modern furniture classics and aspiring classics.

Furniture Shoppers (www.furnitureshoppers.com)
Online store offering one of the Internet's largest selections of contemporary casual and occasional furniture, lighting and accessories.

Furniturefind.com (www.furniturefind.com)
Currently offering the largest selection of furniture online with over one hundred furniture brands available.

Go Furniture (www.go-furniture.com)
Their aim is to bring the finest furniture lines and selection directly to the consumer, offering free shipping on most orders.

Gump's San Francisco (www.gumps.com)
A unique and enticing specialty store, featuring Asian, American and European art objects, mastercrafts, and decorative home accessories.

Home Decorators (www.homedecorators.com)
The Home Decorators Collection is a catalog resource for home décor and improvement, providing quality merchandise since 1990.

Homefurnish.com (www.homefurnish.com)
Loads of information about furniture and furnishings for your home, with an online furniture shopping mall.

Homelife (www.ehomelife.com)
Browse Homelife's furniture collections online, and find a store near you.

iHome.com (www.ihome.com)
An online soft home furnishings destination that focuses on offering the widest selection of linens, bedding and other bed & bath accessories online.

ihomedecor.com (www.ihomedecor.com)
Showcasing a wide variety of home accessories, including Asian, seaside, urban, country, and holiday collections.

IKEA (www.ikea.com)
Offering modern and stylish furnishings that combine good design, good function and good quality at affordable prices.

J. C. Penney (www.jcpenney.com)
The department store offers a broad selection of furnishings and home accessories online.

Kasala (www.kasala.com)
Modern furnishings to delight, surprise, and refresh.

K-Mart (www.bluelight.com)
Home of the Martha Stewart Everyday collections of bed and bath linens and accessories.

L.L. Bean (www.llbean.com)
Offering home furnishings and accessories that reflect a passion for the outdoors.

Lancaster County Market (www.lancastercounty-market.com)
Online market featuring Amish-made products such as furniture, art, and quilts from Lancaster County, Pennsylvania.

Martha Stewart Home (www.marthastewart.com)
Shop for Martha's licensed home products online.

Natural Spaces (www.naturalspaces.com)
Create elegant, unique surroundings with accessories and gifts from Natural Spaces, which offers products made from recycled and natural, sustainable materials.

Neiman Marcus (www.neimanmarcus.com)
Shop for fine furnishings and collectibles online from the venerable department store.

Oriac Design (www.bnu.de/oriac/)
Online catalog offering designer furniture and accessories.

Pendleton Home (www.pendleton-usa.com)
Their product line includes their world-famous blankets, as well as rustic furnishings.

Pier One Imports (www.pier1.com)
Shop online, find out about in-store sales and sign up for their gift registry.

Platypus (www.platypusonline.com)
Platypus's website features some of the store's most popular home furnishings and distinguished gifts.

Pottery Barn (www.potterybarn.com)
Shop for furnishings and accessories, request a catalog, and access their online design guide.

Rainbee (www.rainbee.com)
Designer children's store, featuring furniture and room décor.

Restoration Hardware (www.restorationhardware.com)
Shop for furnishings and home accessories online, request a catalog, or find a retail store near you.

Retrospect (www.retrospecthome.com)
Catalog featuring a collection of home furnishings that brings together timeless design, skilled craftsmanship and fine materials at an outstanding value.

Room & Board (www.roomandboard.com)
Browse and shop for furnishings, and consult with an online design associate before making your purchases.

Rooms to Go (www.roomstogo.com)
International furniture chain offering the latest styles and trends, best prices and fastest delivery on the web.

Shabby Chic (www.shabbychic.com)
Shop for Shabby Chic furnishings and accessories online, or locate a retail location near you.

Smith and Hawken (www.smithandhawken.com)
A leader in gardening products, Smith and Hawken offers a surprisingly large number of furnishings for both the home and the garden.

Southampton Marketplace (www.shampton.com)
Offers slipcovers, area rugs, curtains, and a variety of other home accessories at discounted prices.

Spiegel (www.spiegel.com)
Shop for home furnishings and accessories from one of the nation's leading direct marketers.

Sundance (www.sundancecatalog.com)
Browse and shop for furniture and home décor in Sundance's online catalog.

Sure Fit, Inc. (www.surefit.net)
America's largest furniture cover manufacturer, offering ready-made slipcovers for couches and chairs.

Target (www.target.com)
One of the nation's leading discount retailers, you can shop for a number of Target's home accessories online.

10thAvenue.com (www.10thavenue.com)
A marketplace for the finer things in life, offering a selection of home accents.

Thomasville Furniture (www.thomasville.com)
Furniture manufacturer with dedicated galleries in more than 400 independent retail furniture stores and almost 100 Thomasville Home Furnishing stores across America.

Traditions at Home (www.traditionsathome.com)
The online division of Traditions Furniture, Traditions at Home offers something for every taste and style—from Mission-style furniture and tables to Tiffany lamps and fine area rugs.

Unica (www.unicahome.com)
Offers unique modern accessories for the home, including lighting, vintage ceramics, and new and vintage art glass.

Urban Outfitters (www.urbanoutfitters.com)
Find the latest in casual furnishings and home accessories here. Shop online or locate a retail store near you.

Warm Biscuit (www.warmbiscuit.com)
Offers bedding and furnishings for children's rooms.

Waverly Home (www.waverly.com)
Offers everything you need to express your style. They provide at-home and in-store consultations, as well as a full range of products and services online for a complete and convenient shopping experience.

West Tenth (www.westtenth.com)
Stylish boutique offering unique furnishings and accessories for the home.

Westpoint Stevens (www.westpointstevens.com)

Shop for bedding and bath products online, or find a retailer near you.

Retailers – Flooring

Carpet One (www.carpetone.com)

Comprehensive website for the retail chain, which offers online buying and a carpet-care guide.

Carpet Values (www.carpetvalues.com)

Shop for area rugs and name your own price for carpet.

Cost Less Carpet (www.costlesscarpet.com)

Online carpet superstore where you can order samples before you buy.

Couristan (www.couristan.com)

Known for having the most exquisite handmade and power-loomed floor coverings available anywhere in the world.

Fast Floors (www.fastfloors.com)

Offers a number of options for flooring, with free advice from flooring specialists and more products, information, and services than on any other flooring site on the web.

FloorShop (www.floorshop.com)

Offers a huge selection of flooring options, with an automated system that will provide you with instant price quotes.

Formica (www.formica.com)

Solutions for flooring and countertops, includes online magazine with ideas.

Hosking Hardwood (www.hoskinghardwood.com)

Quality hardwood flooring, from the flooring consultants at This Old House.

iFloor (www.ifloor.com)

Shop online at the most comprehensive flooring website, offering over 40,000 products.

Rugs Online (www.rugsonline.com)

Shop for a number of rug collections online.

S&S Mills (www.ssmills.com)
America's number one resource for buying carpet direct for over 25 years.

Retailers – Lighting

Light Warehouse (www.lightwarehouse.com)
With over fifteen years in the lighting industry, Light Warehouse offers a variety of lighting solutions online.

Lighting Store USA (www.lightingstoreusa.com)
The first Internet-only lighting showroom, offering a number of leading brands at discounted prices.

Lighting Universe (www.lightinguniverse.com)
Offers over 90,000 lighting products for sale online.

Tin Bin (www.thetinbin.com)
Offering eighteenth-century lighting reproductions, including chandeliers, sconces, and lanterns.

Retailers – Windows & Walls

American Blind & Wallpaper Factory (www.abwf.com)
Providing blinds, wallpaper, wall art, and a number of other products for the home.

Blinds 2 You (www.blinds2you.com)
Offers a wide variety of blinds and other window coverings at low prices.

EPaintStore.com (www.epaintstore.com)
Shop online for paint, wallpaper, and accessories.

Sherwin-Williams (www.sherwinwilliams.com)
Offers a huge amount of information for do-it-yourselfers, including advice and recommendations for painting and wallpapering.

Smith & Noble (www.smithandnoble.com)
America's leading resource for window treatments, featuring online ordering, information on measuring and installing, and design assistance.

Furniture Makers & Manufacturers

Look for furnishings from these makers at a retailer near you, or check their websites to learn where to find their products locally.

Ashley Furniture (www.ashleyfurniture.com)

Barlow Tyrie (www.teak.com)

Bassett Furniture (www.bassettfurniture.com)

Bauer International(www.bauerinternational.com)

Berkline (www.berkline.com)

Brown Jordan (www.brownjordanfurniture.com)

Century Furniture (www.centuryfurniture.com)

Councill Companies (www.councill.com)

Guy Chaddock & Co. (www.guychaddock.com)

Habersham Furniture Company (www.habershamdesigns.com)

Henredon (www.henredon.com)

Hooker Furniture (www.hookerfurniture.com)

Kimball Home Furniture (www.kimballhome.com)

Kohler Company (www.kohlerco.com)

Lane Furniture (www.lanefurniture.com)

LA-Z-BOY (www.lazboy.com)

Lexington Home Furnishings (www.lexington.com)

Maitland-Smith (www.maitland-smith.com)

Mulholland Brothers (www.mulhollandbrothers.com)

Pulaski Furniture (www.pulaskifurniture.com)

Sauder Woodworking (www.sauder.com)

Segusino/Marina's (www.segusino.com/ing)

Stanley Furniture Company (www.stanleyfurniture.com)

Susan Sargent Designs (www.susansargent.com)

Vanguard Furniture Company (www.veryvanguard.com)

YAYO! Designs (www.yayodesigns.com)

Zencraft (www.zencraft.com)

Antiques & Collectibles

Circline (www.circline.com)

E-Hammer (www.ehammer.com)

Great Gatsby's (www.greatgatsbys.com)

Icollector.com (www.icollector.com)

Peddle It (www.peddleit.com)

Online Thrift and Flea-Market Shopping

Amazon.com Auctions (www.amazon.com)

City Auction (www.cityauction.com)

Ebay (www.ebay.com)

Excite Outlet Center (outletcenter.excite.com)

Goodwill (www.shopgoodwill.com)

Hotel Surplus Outlet (www.hotelsurplus.com)

Lycos Auctions (auctions.lycos.com)

MSN Auctions (auctions.msn.com)

NBCi Auctions (auctions.nbci.com)

Do-It-Yourself Resources

Bob Vila Home Site (www.bobvila.com)

DoItYourself.com (www.doityourself.com)

Do It Yourself Network (www.diynet.com)

HGTV (www.hgtv.com)

Home Depot (www.homedepot.com)

Hometime (www.hometime.com)

ImproveNet (www.improvenet.com)

Lowe's (www.lowes.com)

Online Shopping Directories

Decorating Studio (www.decoratingstudio.com)

Designviews (www.designviews.com)

FloorFacts (www.floorfacts.com)

Floorsearch (www.floorsearch.com)

FurnitureFan (www.furniturefan.com)

Home Portfolio (www.homeportfolio.com)

Homestore (www.homestore.com)

Kitchen-Bath.com (www.kitchen-bath.com)

World Floor Covering Association (www.wfca.org)

Yahoo! Shopping (shopping.yahoo.com)

Media Resources

Apartment Life (www.apartmentlife.com)

Architectural Digest (www.archdigest.com)

Better Homes & Gardens (www.betterhomes-andgardens.com)

Christopher Lowell Show (dsc.discovery.com/dscdaytime/christopherlowell/christopherlowell.html)

Country Home (www.countryhomemagazine.com)

Country Living (www.countryliving.com)

Designviews (www.designviews.com)

Digs Magazine (www.digsmagazine.com)

Dwell (www.dwellmag.com)

HomeDecoratingSite.com (www.homedecoratingsite.com)

House Beautiful (www.housebeautiful.com)

LivingHome (www.livinghome.com)

LivingRoom Magazine (www.livingroommag.com)

Martha Stewart Living (www.marthastewart.com)

Metropolitan Home (www.methome.com)

Today's Homeowner (www.todayshomeowner.com)

Traditional Home's DesignerFinder (www.designerfinder.com)

Photo credits for resource guide: pp. 146, 149, 153, 155: Photos courtesy of Kozyhome; p. 150: Photo courtesy of Councill Furniture; p. 154: Photo courtesy of Bombay Company.